QUICK LEGAL TERMINOLOGY

QUICK LEGAL TERMINOLOGY

RANDOLPH Z. VOLKELL, J.D.

John Wiley & Sons, Inc.
New York · Chichester · Brisbane · Toronto

Editors: Judy Wilson and Irene Brownstone
Editorial/Production Supervision: Service to Publishers, Inc.

Library of Congress Cataloging in Publication Data

Volkell, Randolph Z.   1950–
    Quick legal terminology.
    (Wiley self-teaching guides)
    Includes index.
    1. Law—United States—Terms and phrases.
2. Law—United States—Programmed instruction.
I. Title.
KF156.V64   340'.0973   79-13647
ISBN 0-471-03786-9

Printed in the United States of America

79   80   10 9 8 7 6 5 4 3 2 1

For Mom and Dad

Foreword

Law is much too important to be left to lawyers. Lawyers have succeeded, however, in establishing a monopoly over law by inventing a language of their own which effectively precludes nonlawyers from learning very much about what it is that lawyers do. As long as conversations about law are conducted in a private code known only to lawyers, their status as monopolists will be secure. Of course, lawyers are not the first interest group to use jargon as a device to shield their activities from outside scrutiny and competition. Elites and would-be elites have typically evolved complex language structures as a means to preserve and enhance their status and power. Books like this one, which demystify professional jargon and threaten to break the lawyers' private code, are serious threats to the *status quo.* After all, when John Wyclyffe translated the Bible into the vernacular and broke the clergy's private code, he was burned and thrown into the Thames. When Jeremy Bentham sought to replace complex common law pleadings with uniform, simplified forms, he was threatened with contempt. I do not expect Randy Volkell to be burned (at least in this life) or thrown into the Hudson. I do expect, however, that books like this will send a wave of unease through Bar Associations everywhere. If people reduce legal terminology to understandable English, it will be possible for the bulk of the population to ask serious questions about law and lawyers and to demand understandable answers. Demystification is the first step to rational discourse. Books like this are welcome indeed.

Burt Neuborne
Professor, School of Law
New York University
New York, New York
July 1979

Acknowledgments

I would like to thank the following people for their invaluable assistance and support:

Elizabeth Boehm, Irene Brownstone, Joyce Campbell,
Michael Ferry, Jacqueline Gilbert, Martha Jewett, Mark Kalman,
Burt Neuborne, Robert Raciti, Merton Reichler, John P. Reid,
Maron Salkin, Robert Volkell, Theresa Volkell, Joshua Wallace,
and Judy Wilson.

RANDY VOLKELL

Contents

QUICK LEGAL
TERMINOLOGY

CROCK

by Bill Rechin & Brant Parker

CROCK by Rechin, Parker & Wilder.
© Field Enterprises, Inc., 1978.
Courtesy of Field Newspaper Syndicate.

Introduction

The purpose of this book is to introduce you to the language of the law. The statements about the law are very general, going only as deep as is necessary to introduce the terminology of each legal area. Lawyers have a reputation for being hard to understand. While the modern trend is to make the language of the law more comprehensible to the layman, a large number of technical words are still not familiar to most people outside the legal profession. Our goal is not to teach you the law but to familiarize you with some of the key words and concepts of the law.

The law takes many forms. It may, for example, be enacted by a legislature, or it may evolve as part of the common law (judge-made law). The function of the courts is always to interpret legislation and even the Constitution, the supreme law of the land. American justice is administered through several systems of courts. Each state, as well as the federal government, has its own judicial network. In some cases, the federal courts have supremacy over the state courts; in others, the state courts are sovereign, or autonomous.

Put most simply, each system has three basic levels of courts: a large number of trial courts at the lowest level, a group of intermediate appellate courts, and one high court which has the power to make a final, definitive ruling. In the federal system, the first level is made up of ninety district courts, with at least one district in each state. The federal system also includes eleven intermediate appellate courts, called courts of appeals (formerly called circuit courts), and one Supreme Court, which has the final word. Appeal from a district court to an appellate court is generally allowed as a matter of right but, depending on the case, appeal to the Supreme Court may only be had by permission of that court. This permission is requested by a writ of certiorari, which will be granted if four of the nine justices (judges) of the Supreme Court vote in favor of it.

Many states use different names to describe the three levels of courts. In New York, for example, the lower-level courts are called "Supreme Courts";

the Supreme Court has four Appellate Divisions, which form the intermediate appellate level; and the highest court is called the Court of Appeals.

The law can be divided into two vast areas: adjective (procedural) law and substantive law. Adjective or procedural law governs the carrying out of a case in court, and includes the rules of both civil and criminal procedure and the rules of evidence. The initial procedural question in any case, of course, is deciding where to bring the action. Centuries ago, in England, because of the nature of the legal system, the law was often unable to provide an adequate remedy. The Chancellor (Sir Thomas More was probably the most famous Chancellor) was then called upon to decree an equitable remedy. A system of courts of equity evolved, taking over whenever there was no adequate remedy at law. Today, the two systems of courts have merged into one. Now, questions of "which court should I sue in" are more likely to involve a choice between state and federal court or the courts of two different states. Resolution of actual conflicts of laws between systems is a highly complex field which we will not explore.

The part of the law that deals with the actual rights of the parties to a suit is known as substantive law. It, too, is divided into various areas of study. The subject of constitutional law is important, as all laws must be measured against the Constitution. If a law is found to be unconstitutional, that law cannot stand. In this book, we will deal, at least briefly, with many areas of the substantive law, such as torts and criminal law.

As you read through the book, key words will be italicized when they are first introduced. If you want to know more about the meaning of a word than the discussion provides, look up the word in the Glossary at the back of the book. (For still more detail, you may wish to refer to a good law dictionary, such as Ballentine's or Black's.) The material is presented in numbered sections called frames. At the end of each frame will be at least one review question to give you practice in applying legal terms, with the answer given below a line of dashes. The goal of each chapter is to achieve a basic knowledge of the vocabulary of the subject covered. The Glossary, which contains all the key words from the chapters and many more as well, will serve as a permanent reference for legal terminology.

At the end of each chapter is a brief self-test which should indicate what you have learned and what you need to review. You might wish to wait a while between finishing the chapter and taking the test, so that you can see how much you have actually retained. A final self-test is also provided for that purpose.

Don't try to rush through this book; take your time and remember to look up any words you are not sure of. In that way, you will learn the key terms and concepts of legal terminology most effectively.

CHAPTER ONE

Civil Procedure

The purpose of a system of courts is to administer the rules and regulations propounded by society. Over the years, the courts themselves found it necessary to develop rules of procedure. This chapter deals with the rules of civil procedure.

1. An *action* is any *judicial* (or *court*) *proceeding. Civil actions* include all court actions that do not involve criminal law. They are generally carried on by one individual or corporation against another. Most people are familiar with the names given to the litigants or participants in a lawsuit —the person who brings the action is called the *plaintiff* and the person being sued is the *defendant.* The purpose of the action may be to redress some wrong or to vindicate some right, and the action itself may involve a contract, a tort, some property, or other matter. Each of these will be discussed in some detail in the appropriate chapter. In the federal system and in each state system, both civil and criminal cases are handled. In this chapter, we will be concerned with the subject of civil *procedure*, the rules that govern the carrying on of a civil action in court.

   What is a civil action?

   _ _ _ _ _ _ _ _ _ _ _ _

   A civil action is any judicial (or court) proceeding that does not involve criminal law.

2. The first question to be considered in bringing an action is whether the court has *jurisdiction* to hear the case. In its broadest sense, jurisdiction is the right of the court to exercise its power. The power to handle a

specific type of case is called *subject matter jurisdiction*. In addition to subject matter jurisdiction, the court must have jurisdiction over the parties to the lawsuit, or *in personam* jurisdiction. In certain cases, the only issue is the ownership or status of a particular property (such as land). Then the court must have *in rem* jurisdiction, or jurisdiction over the property. There is also *quasi in rem* jurisdiction, which also involves a determination of rights to some property, but only between the parties to the suit.

Where the court would not otherwise have jurisdiction, the defendant may still consent in some way to being sued. Consent may be implied rather than expressed. For example, a corporation may be held to consent to being sued in a state when it engages in business within the state. A law that extends the jurisdiction of the state to people outside its borders is called a *long-arm statute*.

(a) If Canute sues Baldi to recover for injuries he suffered when Baldi punched him, what kind(s) of jurisdiction would the court need?

_____ subject matter
_____ in personam
_____ in rem
_____ quasi in rem

(b) If the Wallace County Civil Court has jurisdiction to hear cases up to a maximum of $1,000, and Mr. Brent brings an action to recover the $2,000 he loaned Mr. Case, the court

_____ has jurisdiction.
_____ lacks subject matter jurisdiction.
_____ lacks in personam jurisdiction.
_____ lacks quasi in rem jurisdiction.

(c) If the court of Mahzjeauneszz County has no personal jurisdiction over Mr. Kathroo, is there any way for Mr. Jefferson to sue him in that court? Explain.

_ _ _ _ _ _ _ _ _ _ _ _ _

(a) Subject matter and in personam. The court needs jurisdiction over Baldi and the type of case.

(b) The court lacks subject matter jurisdiction. It can only hear cases up to $1,000 and this case does not fall within that limit.

(c) Yes. Mr. Kathroo could consent to be sued.

3. The filing of the suit is just one step in commencing an action. An equally important requirement is that the defendant receive *notice* of the action. This is usually done by serving him with a *summons*, a paper which serves the dual purpose of notifying the defendant and invoking the court's jurisdiction.

Service of *process* (the delivery of the summons to the defendant) may take one of several acceptable forms, depending upon the circumstances of the particular case. *Personal service* requires that the defendant actually be handed a copy of the summons; *substituted service*, where appropriate, allows the summons to be handed to someone else for the defendant; and *constructive service*, which is only used in limited circumstances, allows actions such as mailing or publishing notice for the defendant.

Where the case involves some property of a defendant, the court may be able to obtain jurisdiction over the property even when it is unable to invoke personal jurisdiction over the defendant (for example, if the defendant cannot be served properly with process). Property within the jurisdiction may be attached. *Attachment*, pursuant to a statute, is a seizure of some of the defendant's property to be sold and the money used to pay off, for example, the defendant's debt to the plaintiff. Some form of notice, of course, must be given to the defendant.

Attachment is useful where the subject of the suit is *tangible* (subject to physical touching and possession). Where *intangibles* are involved, the analogous remedy of *garnishment* may be appropriate. For example, a debt may be garnished by serving process on the *debtor.* One of the key values of garnishment is its use in a direct action against an insurance company in case of an accident.

(a) What are the two purposes of serving a summons?

(b) Serving process through the mail is

_____ perfectly acceptable and proper.
_____ only valid as notice to the defendant.
_____ never acceptable.
_____ allowed only in certain circumstances.

(c) If Maron's car is hit by an out-of-state motorist (upon whom she is unable to serve process), how might she commence an action to recover damages?

(d) What are intangibles?

_ _ _ _ _ _ _ _ _ _ _ _

(a) To invoke the jurisdiction of the court and to notify the defendant.

(b) It is a form of constructive service, and is allowed only in certain circumstances.

(c) She could garnish the insurance policy by serving process on the other motorist's insurance company.

(d) Things with value but no physical substance (such as debts and insurance policies).

4. *Federal* Courts have special jurisdictional problems. They have original subject matter jurisdiction only in certain cases. The most natural, of course, is in a case where a *federal question* is involved. The constitutional definition of a case involving a federal question is one that "arises under the Constitution, laws or treaties of the United States." The second major area of federal jurisdiction is in a case where there is *diversity of citizenship* between the parties. The most common cases of diversity are suits between citizens of different states, or suits involving foreign citizens. In both cases (federal question and diversity) the amount in controversy must be greater than a specific *jurisdictional* amount. The jurisdictional amount currently required is anything in excess of $10,000.

> Could one New York resident sue another New York resident in Federal Court as long as the suit was for an amount in excess of $10,000? Explain.

> _ _ _ _ _ _ _ _ _ _ _ _

> Maybe, if a federal question were involved. There is no diversity of citizenship.

5. Sometimes several courts may have jurisdiction over a particular case. The question of *venue* involves the selection of the court in which the action will be initiated. It is often a question of convenience. Venue may lie where the defendant lives, where the plaintiff lives, or where the

cause of action (the underlying reason for the lawsuit) arose, to name a few possibilities. If land is involved, venue usually lies in the county where the land is situated. It is generally up to the plaintiff to select the venue, since it is he who brings the action. However, if the plaintiff selects a *forum* (court) that is extremely inconvenient for the defendant, the court may, if it so chooses, decline to hear the case. The doctrine that allows this is called *forum non conveniens* (inconvenient forum), and it is entirely discretionary with the court.

(a) What is a cause of action?

(b) How could the doctrine of forum non conveniens be useful in a challenge to a court's jurisdiction? Explain.

_ _ _ _ _ _ _ _ _ _ _ _ _ _

(a) The facts giving rise to the right to start a lawsuit or the right itself.

(b) It couldn't. Forum non conveniens only deals with venue; the court is assumed to have jurisdiction before the doctrine comes into play.

6. It is possible for several plaintiffs to join their cases against one defendant (or for one plaintiff to join several cases of his own); either way, this is called *joinder*. In some cases, where a large enough group of plaintiffs all have similar causes of action, they might proceed with what is called a *class action*, a procedural device that allows a small group of named plaintiffs to act on behalf of a larger group, all with similar causes of action. Some class actions involve the rights of thousands of class members.

While the original claim in the case is that of the plaintiff against the defendant, the defendant is allowed to *counterclaim*, or raise his own claim, against the plaintiff. In a case with more than one defendant, if one defendant has a claim against another defendant, he can raise it in what is called a *cross-claim*. The parties involved in a case are not necessarily limited to the original litigants; a third party who has a legitimate interest in the outcome of the case may be allowed to enter the suit voluntarily. This is called *intervention*. If a party already involved feels it necessary, a third party can sometimes be *impleaded*, or brought into the suit after it is under way.

(a) When would it be appropriate for the plaintiff to cross-claim?

(b) If Mr. Maroni is suing Mr. Salkinetti for the rights to a boat which, in fact, is owned by Mr. Betherman, how can Mr. Betherman most appropriately assert his rights?

_____ intervention
_____ impleader (the act of impleading)
_____ counterclaim
_____ cross-claim

– – – – – – – – – – – –

(a) Never. Only defendants may cross-claim (even if there are several plaintiffs).

(b) Mr. Betherman can assert his rights through intervention. The lawsuit between the others is already in progress. Intervention is the only procedure that allows a third party to join the suit voluntarily; the other three choices can only be initiated by someone who is already a party to the suit.

7. Before a case ever comes to trial, it goes through a stage called *pleading.* Each side pleads, thereby notifying the other of the basic nature of its case and clarifying what the issues will be. The first pleading is the *complaint*, which explains the plaintiff's cause of action and demands some relief, as well as identifying the parties. It also includes some *allegations*, or assertions, of fact. The defendant's first pleading is the *answer.* The answer may take the form of a *denial*, a repudiation of the claims made in the complaint; it may, instead, set forth some *affirmative defenses;* or both. For example, if Felix sued Oscar, claiming that Oscar punched him, an affirmative defense might be that Felix had punched Oscar first and that Oscar, therefore, had acted in self-defense. In some cases the plaintiff may file a *reply* to the defendant's answer.
   Pleadings can generally be *amended*, and if additional facts come to light after a pleading is filed, a *supplemental pleading* may be used to bring them to the court's attention. Any application to the court for a ruling (either during the pleadings or later) is called a *motion.* A motion for *summary judgment*, for example, is a motion that the court award judgment to the plaintiff on the grounds that the defendant has offered patently insufficient evidence to controvert the plaintiff's case. The analogous remedy for the defendant would be a motion to *dismiss*, or

order the lawsuit ended, because the plaintiff failed to present a *prima facie case.* In order to present a prima facie case, the plaintiff must put forward enough evidence to establish his claim if there were no defense evidence. The motion to dismiss is a modern device created by statute. Its common law equivalent was called a *demurrer.* The demurrer assumed everything in the complaint to be true, and claimed that there was still no basis for any recovery by the plaintiff.

(a) Faced with an insufficient complaint, a defendant should

_____ file an amended complaint.
_____ file a supplemental complaint.
_____ file a demurrer.
_____ move for a summary judgment.
_____ move to dismiss.

(b) What is an affirmative defense?

(c) Which of the following might a plaintiff properly do?

_____ move to dismiss
_____ file a reply
_____ file a demurrer
_____ file an answer
_____ move for summary judgment

— — — — — — — — — — — — — —

(a) Move to dismiss. A demurrer would have been the correct remedy at common law.

(b) It is a defense other than a mere denial; it brings forth new issues, and therefore might be successful even if plaintiff's claims are all true.

(c) A plaintiff might file a reply or move for summary judgment. The others choices would be actions of a defendant.

8. There are two types of issues in any case: issues of law and issues of fact. The judge always has the responsibility for deciding the legal issues; the factual issues are always the province of the trier of fact. In many cases, the Constitution guarantees a *jury* to try the facts, although this right can be waived, in which case the judge becomes the trier of fact. In cases where there is a jury, the judge instructs it on the law, but the jury makes its own decision about the facts.

The trial itself begins with the *opening statements* of the opposing lawyers, in which each side gives an outline of what it plans to prove. Then, the *evidence* is presented. Presentation of evidence is governed by a complex set of rules that we will deal with in Chapter 2. Once all the evidence has been heard, the lawyers make their *summations*, or closing statements, in which they argue their case to the jury or the judge, whoever is the trier of fact in the case. In case of a jury trial, the judge then instructs, or *charges*, the jury on the law. Finally, the trier of fact retires to deliberate, and eventually reaches a *verdict.*

Which of the following is (are) the responsibility of a jury?

_____ determining the facts
_____ determining the law
_____ making a summation
_____ rendering a verdict

– – – – – – – – – – – – –

The jury determines the facts and renders a verdict. The law is the province of the judge, and summations are made by the attorneys.

9. The final determination in the case is called the *judgment.* It is pro- nounced by the judge at the end of the case (if there is a jury, after they have reached their verdict). The doctrine of *res judicata* states that the final judgment of the court is binding on the parties; they cannot con- duct another suit to try the same cause of action again. This doctrine is often confused with that of *collateral estoppel.* While res judicata pre- vents any further litigation on the same cause of action, collateral estoppel deals only with points actually dealt with in the first litigation, preventing litigation of those points in a new cause of action. For example, in a bus accident, suppose that one passenger sues and the driver is found not to be negligent. Under res judicata, the passenger cannot file another suit later relating to the same case. Collateral estoppel makes that ruling binding on any other passenger who sues.

   When a litigant is not satisfied with the judgment rendered by a trial court, he has the option of taking an *appeal* to a higher court. An appeal is a *review* of the record of the case, to determine if any errors were made in the lower court that require the decision in the case to be *reversed.* In each system of courts, there are generally several inter- mediate appellate courts and one high court of appeal that has the final word.

Mr. Eccles is involved in an automobile accident and he sues the other party (and wins) for injuries he suffered to his leg. Can he later sue for injuries to his arm? Explain.

— — — — — — — — — — — —

No. The doctrine of res judicata prevents a second suit on the original cause of action (the accident).

CHAPTER 1 SELF-TEST

The following questions will help you test your understanding of the terms and concepts in this chapter. Check your answers with those that follow the test. If they do not agree, you may want to review the appropriate part of the chapter.

1. If a case were brought in a state court against a nonresident who was not at the time and had never been in the state, the case would be dismissed for lack of _____ jurisdiction.

   _____ in personam
   _____ in rem
   _____ quasi in rem
   _____ subject matter

2. What does a summons accomplish?

3. What is the key difference between attachment and garnishment?

4. Failure to meet the jurisdictional amount in federal court is a problem of _____ jurisdiction.

   _____ in personam
   _____ in rem
   _____ quasi in rem
   _____ subject matter

5. The doctrine of forum non conveniens might be used to change

   _____ the jurisdiction.
   _____ the venue.
   _____ the residence of the defendant.
   _____ the residence of the plaintiff.

6. Which of the following might be done by a plaintiff in a case?

   _____ counterclaim
   _____ cross-claim
   _____ intervention
   _____ impleader

7. What are two purposes of pleading?

8. What are the two types of issues in any case?

9. What is the difference between res judicata and collateral estoppel?

10. Does a party against whom a judgment is rendered have any further recourse? Explain.

ANSWERS

1. In personam. Even a long-arm statute could not reach such a person.

2. It invokes the jurisdiction of the court and notifies the defendant.

3. Attachment refers to tangibles; garnishment to intangibles.

4. Subject matter. The Federal Court can only hear certain cases if the amount in controversy exceeds $10,000.

5. The venue.

6. Impleader. Either party can implead a third party. Counterclaim and cross-claim are available only to defendants, intervention only to an outsider.

7. To clarify the issues and notify the opponents.

8. Law and fact.

9. Res judicata prevents further litigation on the same cause of action; collateral estoppel prevents further litigation about the same issue.

10. Yes. He can appeal.

CHAPTER TWO

Evidence

Perhaps the most important courtroom rules are the rules governing what information, or evidence, the parties to the suit are allowed to bring to the court's attention. This chapter deals with these rules of evidence.

1. Once a trial is in progress, the rules of *evidence* govern what evidence (or information) is to be heard in determining the truth. The three most basic requirements for evidence to be *admissible* are that it be *competent*, *relevant*, and *material*. Evidence is material if it relates to one of the issues in the case. It is relevant if it is in some way helpful in determining the truth about the issue to which it relates. Finally, it is competent if it does not violate any of the rules of evidence that might make it inadmissible.

   Evidence may be *direct*, proving the fact without reference to other facts, or *circumstantial*, offering *proof* by implication.

   (a) Is material evidence always admissible? Explain.

   (b) If you wanted to prove that it was raining, what kind of evidence would it be that people were carrying open umbrellas?

   _ _ _ _ _ _ _ _ _ _ _ _ _

   (a) No. It might be irrelevant or incompetent.

   (b) Circumstantial evidence. Evidence that people were getting wet would be more direct.

2. Information can come before a court in several ways. The first is by *judicial notice*, the recognition by the court that certain facts are true

even though they have not been presented as evidence. Such facts are generally either common knowledge or just very easy to verify. Of course, courts ordinarily take judicial notice of laws.

Testimony, the verbal evidence given by witnesses, is the best known form of evidence, but evidence may also be *real* or *documentary*. Where real evidence is used, the actual object in question is presented for the trier of fact to inspect. Documentary evidence involves the use of something in written form. The *parol evidence rule* states that when an agreement has been put in writing, only the writing itself can be used as evidence of the agreement (see contracts in Chapter Four).

(a) What type of evidence is involved in a court's recognition of the fact that Thomas Jefferson was the third President of the United States? Explain.

(b) What type of evidence might involve no words, either written or spoken?

— — — — — — — — — — — —

(a) No evidence is involved. The court would take judicial notice of it.

(b) Real evidence. Testimony involves spoken evidence and documentary evidence is written.

3. In order to give testimony, a *witness* must be *competent.* Witnesses are assumed to be competent unless they are shown to be otherwise. To be a competent witness, a person must have had the ability to observe whatever it is he is to testify to. He must also be able to remember it and communicate it to others. Finally, he must take an *oath* and appreciate the obligation to be truthful.

The party who calls a witness has the first opportunity to question him. This is called *direct examination*, and proceeds with the attorney eliciting information from the witness by asking questions. If the opposing attorney feels that the testimony being given is inadmissible or that a question is improper, he can *object.* If the judge agrees that the question is improper, the *objection* will be *sustained*, and the witness will not be allowed to answer. The objection might also be *overruled*, in which case the witness will be allowed to answer.

An example of an improper question on direct examination might be a

Source: B.C.; by permission of Johnny Hart and Field Enterprises, Inc.

leading question, one in which the lawyer basically gives the testimony, suggesting the desired answer (which will probably be a simple "yes" or "no"). Leading questions are not, however, always improper. They are allowed, for example, on direct examination of a *hostile witness*, one whose sympathies lie with the opposing party. In most instances only a qualified *expert witness* can testify as to his opinion.

(a) If a witness is able to remember quite clearly and to communicate to others that at the moment of an accident his view was obscured by a bus, is he competent to testify to the facts of the accident? Explain.

(b) A lawyer asks a witness, "And next, did you knock on the door twice, enter the aprtment, and find the stuffed cookie monster on the chair?" On what grounds might his adversary object?

— — — — — — — — — — — —

(a) No. By his own testimony, he did not have an opportunity to observe the event.

(b) It is a leading question.

4. After the direct examination of a witness has been completed, the opposing party has a right to *cross-examine* the witness. Leading questions are permitted on cross-examination, but the scope of the questioning is limited to matters dealt with in the direct examination and matters relating to the credibility of the witness.
    Any attempt to discredit the witness is known as *impeachment.*

Although a party is not allowed to impeach his own witness, there are several acceptable ways to impeach an opponent's witness. One might show that the witness was for some reason unable to perceive the event in question. Assuming that the witness was able to observe, it is possible to offer a reason why he might not be giving a truthful account, either because he has a reputation for being untruthful; he is biased or interested in the case; he has made a prior statement that is inconsistent with his testimony; he has been convicted of a crime; or he has committed some other act that might affect his credibility.

(a) Mr. Roberts is suing Mr. Michaels. Mr. Roberts' attorney calls Mr. Stevens as a witness. Which of the following reasons can he use to impeach Mr. Stevens?

_____ Mr. Stevens was once convicted of fraud.
_____ A week before the trial, Mr. Stevens told Ms. Gilbert the opposite of what he is now testifying.
_____ Mr. Stevens is the brother-in-law of his opponent.
_____ Mr. Stevens is known as a liar.
_____ Mr. Stevens beats his wife.

(b) Which of the reasons given above could Mr. Michaels use in his cross-examination if he wanted to impeach Mr. Stevens?

_ _ _ _ _ _ _ _ _ _ _ _ _

(a) None. Mr. Roberts called Mr. Stevens as his own witness.

(b) All of them. They are all proper grounds for impeachment of a witness.

5. Probably the most famous type of excluded evidence is *hearsay*. Hearsay is an out-of-court statement offered as proof of what is asserted in the statement. The party offering the statement is the *proponent*. Obviously, when a statement made by a person who is not present in court is introduced, it is impossible for the opposing party to cross-examine the *declarant* (the person who originally made the statement). In addition, accuracy may be lost in two basic ways: the person testifying may not have accurately perceived what the declarant said, or he may not, for some reason, be communicating it accurately.

Many exceptions to the rule against hearsay exist, usually involving some set of facts that tends to make the evidence more necessary or more believable. If the evidence falls within one of the recognized exceptions to the rule, it is admissible. Furthermore, not all out-of-court statements are hearsay. For example, a statement that is not offered to prove the truth of the assertion it contains is not hearsay at all.

(a) If Karla offers to testify that Richard made the statement, "I am King Canute the Bald, ruler of Ohio," is the statement admissible? Explain.

(b) In the example above, who is the declarant? Who is the witness?

- - - - - - - - - - - - - - -

(a) Maybe. If it is offered to prove that Richard was, in fact, King Canute (as asserted in the statement), it may be inadmissible hearsay. If it is offered for some other purpose (e.g., to show that Richard is insane), it is not hearsay at all.

(b) Richard is the declarant and Karla is the witness.

6. There are many exceptions to the hearsay rule. We will deal only with some of the more important ones. An *admission* by one of the parties to the lawsuit is admissible. An admission is any voluntary statement by one party supporting a position taken by the other party. (It need not be against the declarant's own interest at the time that it is made.) For example, Barry hears Arthur say, "I saw Paul being attacked by a falcon." It turns out that Arthur owns the only falcon in the county, and Paul later sues Arthur, whose defense is that Paul was not attacked by a falcon at all, but by a vicious parakeet. Barry can testify as to Arthur's original out-of-court statement, which is now an admission.

An admission should not be confused with a *declaration against interest*, which need not be made by one of the parties. All that matters in the latter is that the declarant be knowingly making a statement that is significantly against his interest at the time of making the statement. For an admission to be admissible evidence, it does not matter if the declarant is available at the trial. A declaration against interest, however, is admissible only if the declarant is not available. Thus, the evidence is necessary (since the declarant is not available) and reliable (why would declarant speak against his own interest if he were speaking falsely?). For example, suppose that Steve is being sued for breaking Mrs. Wilson's window. At trial, a witness testified that he heard Tom, who is now overseas, say "I broke Mrs. Wilson's window." The statement would be admissible as a declaration against interest, since Tom is now unavailable, knew the facts, and was speaking against his own interest.

(a) Which of the following statements must be true for an admission to be admissible evidence even though it is hearsay?

_____ (1) It must be made by a person who is party to the lawsuit.

_____ (2) The declarant must be unavailable at trial.

_____ (3) The statement must be against declarant's interest when it is made.

_____ (4) Declarant must have knowledge of the facts.

(b) Which of the statements above must be true in order for a declaration against interest to be excepted from the hearsay exclusion?

_ _ _ _ _ _ _ _ _ _ _ _ _ _ _

(a) 1 only.

(b) 2, 3, and 4. The declaration against interest need not be made by a party to the lawsuit. It is admissible as long as it is made by a declarant against his own interest at the time of the statement. This means that he must know the facts and know that he is speaking adversely to his own interest. Although an admission is admissible even if the declarant (a party) is available, a declaration against interest can only be used where the declarant is unavailable.

7. Sometimes the circumstances surrounding the making of the statement qualify the statement as an exception to the hearsay rule. One example is the *dying declaration.* A dying declaration may be admissible if made by a person who is in *extremis* (i.e., at the point of death), and knows it. The necessity is obvious: the dead declarant cannot testify later at a trial. The reliability factor is a bit less certain, but historically admission of dying declaration has been justified with the assertion that a man would not want to meet his Maker with a lie on his lips.

Certain spontaneous utterances are also admissible on the theory that if they are spontaneous or excited, they are less likely to be thought out and more likely to be reliable. Records of earlier testimony and records kept in the course of running a business may also be exceptions to the hearsay rule.

Andrews believes he is dying and he accuses Pilner of inflicting the wounds, which he believes to be fatal. He recovers, but dies in a skiing accident before the trial. Does his accusation fit into an exception to the rule against hearsay? Explain.

— — — — — — — — — — — —

No. Although he is unavailable due to death, and he did believe himself to be dying at the time he made the statement, he was not actually in extremis at the time.

CHAPTER 2 SELF-TEST

The following questions will help you test your understanding of the terms and concepts in this chapter. Check your answers with those that follow the test. If they do not agree, you may want to review the appropriate part of the chapter.

1. What are the requirements for admissible evidence?

2. What are three broad classifications of evidence?

3. When are leading questions allowed?

    _____ on direct examination of any witness
    _____ on cross-examination of any witness
    _____ on direct examination of a hostile witness
    _____ on direct examination of an expert witness

4. Which of the following reasons can be used to impeach an opposition witness?

    _____ reputation for untruthfulness
    _____ bias
    _____ interest
    _____ prior bad acts
    _____ prior convictions

5. Which of the reasons above can be used to impeach a party's own witness?

6. If Jane is suing Dick for custody of their dog Spot, and Jane wants to call Martha to testify that Dick said, "I don't like Spot anyway," who is the

    proponent? _____ The declarant? _____

    _____ The witness? _____

7. Would the evidence be admissible? Explain.

8. In a lawsuit arising out of an automobile accident, the driver of one car wants to call as a witness a person who overheard an observer say, "Wow! That guy must be going 100 miles an hour!" in reference to the other car. Is the statement hearsay? Is it admissible? Explain.

ANSWERS

1. It must be competent, relevant, and material.

2. Testimony, real evidence, documentary evidence.

3. On cross-examination of any witness and on direct examination of a hostile witness. Experts are allowed to give opinion evidence, but this does not allow attorneys to ask them leading questions.

4. All may be used to impeach an opposition witness.

5. None. A party may not impeach his own witness.

6. Jane is the proponent, Dick the declarant, and Martha the witness.

7. Probably. It could most likely be classified an admission, since Dick is a party to the suit and now wants custody of Spot.

8. Yes, it is hearsay, but it may be admissible as an excited utterance.

CHAPTER THREE

Torts

Our society has made the judgment that when one person causes harm to another, the person causing the harm should have to compensate the injured party. This chapter deals with the law of torts, or civil wrongs.

1. A *tort* is a wrong or *injury* inflicted on one person by another as a result of a *breach* of an existing legal *duty* or obligation. In tort law, *liability*, or legal responsibility, is usually based on *fault.* If a tort action is successful, two types of *damages* may be recovered. *Compensatory* (or actual) damages are awarded as compensation for the injury. *Punitive* (or exemplary) damages may sometimes be awarded as a penalty where the injury is particularly outrageous. A person who commits a tort is called a *tortfeasor.* When a lawsuit is instituted as a result of a tort, the tortfeasor will be the defendant and the person who has been injured will be the plaintiff.

    (a) If an injury occurs as a result of an inevitable accident, has a tort been committed? Explain.

    (b) If an injury is a result of a mistake, has a tort been committed? Explain.

    (c) Is it possible to recover compensatory damages in excess of the actual injury? Explain.

- - - - - - - - - - - - - - -

(a) No. If the accident was inevitable, no one was at fault.

(b) Yes, if the mistake was a breach of some duty.

(c) No. Any recovery in excess of the actual injury would be punitive or exemplary damages.

2. Many types of torts exist. The first group that we shall consider are called intentional torts. *Intent* is defined as a determination to achieve a particular end by a particular means either because the actor desires the end result or because he acts in such a way that it is practically inevitable. Perhaps the most obvious intentional tort is *battery*, an unlawful touching of one person by another. The touching may be made by the person himself or by some object under his control, but it must be intentional. In order to be considered unlawful, the touching must be in some way offensive or injurious.

   Contact, however, is not necessary in order for a tort to occur. Placing another in fear of imminent physical harm constitutes the intentional tort of *assault*. Words alone are not enough; for there to be assault, some intentional overt act must actually cause the other person to feel frightened.

   False imprisonment, which is the unlawful restraint of one person by another, is also an intentional tort.

   Damage to property as well as injury to the person may constitute an intentional tort.

   Trespass, another tort, is an intentional illegal entry onto the land of another.

   (a) If Doug throws a snowball at Mamie's back and misses, has Doug committed an assault? Explain.

   (b) If he had hit her, would it have been a battery? Explain.

   — — — — — — — — — — — —

   (a) Probably not. A requisite of assault is that the victim be frightened, which is unlikely if the victim does not know what has happened.

   (b) Yes, even if she didn't realize she had been hit. Awareness is not necessary in the case of battery.

3. Certain defenses can be raised by a person who is charged with committing an intentional tort. The two most important are *consent* and *self-defense.* Consent, or voluntary agreement, to the tort may be given expressly or implied. For example, professional football players impliedly give their consent to a large number of batteries every time they play a game. Furthermore, when a person believes that he is about to be attacked, he can use a *reasonable* amount of force to protect himself or others.

    If Dirk thinks that Nasty is about to throw a snowball at him, and he prevents the attack by shooting Nasty in the arm, can he be charged with a tort? Does he have a defense? Explain.

    _ _ _ _ _ _ _ _ _ _ _ _ _

    He can be charged with battery, and he cannot legitimately raise self-defense. Shooting someone is not a reasonable defense against a snowball. Use of excessive force eliminates the defense.

4. Not all torts are intentional; many result from *negligence*, or the failure to exercise proper care under the circumstances. The defendant's conduct is often compared to what would be expected of an imaginary "reasonable man" to determine if the defendant has been negligent. To win a negligence action, the plaintiff must show that defendant had a duty to act in a certain way and that there was a breach of that duty. As a result of the breach, the plaintiff must show that he suffered a loss; the breach must be the immediate or *proximate cause* of plaintiff's damage. The duties that exist depend to a large extent on the relationship of the parties; for example, an owner of a building owes different duties to guests than to trespassers.

    Which of the following is (are) necessary in order for plaintiff to be able to win a negligence action?

    _____ (a) Defendant must have intended the harm.
    _____ (b) Defendant must have acted reasonably.
    _____ (c) Defendant must have breached some duty.
    _____ (d) There must be actual damage.

    _ _ _ _ _ _ _ _ _ _ _ _ _

(c) and (d) In order for there to be a recovery for negligence, some existing duty must be breached, proximately causing some actual damage.

5. In a negligence case, the *burden of proof* is on the plaintiff. The plaintiff must come forward and prove his case. Sometimes this is made extremely difficult by the fact that the defendant has complete control of the evidence. For example, a heavy weight fell out of a window of the defendant's factory and landed on the plaintiff. It is difficult to imagine how the weight fell out of the window without negligence, but it is almost impossible for the plaintiff to prove it without defendant's cooperation. In such a case, plaintiff can invoke the doctrine of *res ipsa loquitur*, which means "the thing itself speaks." The incident itself is considered evidence of negligence.

Defenses in negligence cases include *contributory negligence.* In some states, a plaintiff who is even slightly negligent cannot collect at all. Many states have switched to a *comparative negligence* rule, under which the negligence of both parties is taken into account. *Assumption of risk*, where the plaintiff knows of a risk but decides to take a chance, is another defense. In some states, the party who has the *last clear chance* to avoid the damage is considered to be at fault.

(a) Does the doctrine of res ipsa loquitur shift the burden of proof? Explain.

(b) If Paul and Ellen are involved in an automobile accident, and Ellen was negligent, can Paul recover damages? To what extent? Explain.

— — — — — — — — — — — — —

(a) No. It serves as evidence of negligence, but the burden of proof remains on the plaintiff.

(b) Maybe. First we have to know if Paul was negligent or had the last clear chance. If the answer to either of those questions is affirmative, we would need to know the appropriate rule in the jurisdiction.

6. Sometimes a defendant is held liable for damages even where he cannot actually be shown to be at fault. This is called *strict liability*. For example, people who own wild animals or who engage in extremely hazardous activities may be held liable for damage caused by their animals or activities even if they are not negligent. Strict liability also applies to the sale of products that are "unreasonably dangerous." There is always an *implied warranty* that goods are fit for sale. Where that warranty is breached, strict liability may be applied.

   (a) Mr. H. is trying to bang a nail into the wall with his new hammer. Instead, he bangs his thumb. Does strict liability apply against the manufacturer of the hammer? Explain.

   (b) Would there be strict liability if a piece of the hammer chipped off and hit Mr. H. in the neck, cutting him? Explain.

   _ _ _ _ _ _ _ _ _ _ _ _ _

   (a) No. There is no way to manufacture a hammer that could not hurt a thumb.

   (b) Much more likely. Hammers that chip into small pieces are not fit tools.

7. Torts need not necessarily involve anything physical at all; words alone might be harmful enough to be actionable, as in the case of *defamation*, or injury to the reputation of another. To prove defamation, one must show *defamatory* language by the defendant about the plaintiff. The language must be *published* (made public) to a third person and do damage to the plaintiff's reputation. The defamatory language can be either spoken or written. If spoken, it is called *slander;* if written, it is called *libel.* A written statement that is libel *per se* is actionable even if no damages can be shown. That is, damages are assumed if the statement is libelous on its face, without any extrinsic evidence. Slander is ordinarily not actionable unless damages can be shown, although there are several types of statements that are classified as slander per se.

   Of course, if the defamatory statement is true, the defendant has a complete defense. In some other cases the speaker is said to have a *privilege* that allows him to utter defamatory language without being held liable.

(a) If a presidential candidate makes a slip of the tongue in which he insults an ethnic group, and a newspaper reports the slip, costing the candidate the election, what sort of defamation is the paper guilty of? Explain.

(b) When is a written statement slanderous? Explain.

— — — — — — — — — — — —

(a) None. Remember, truth is a complete defense. In this case, the candidate did make the statement reported.

(b) Never. A written statement that is defamatory is libelous. A spoken defamatory statement is slanderous.

8. To protect themselves against liability, tortious or otherwise, people sometimes purchase *insurance*, a contract under which one party agrees to *indemnify* (secure) another against a certain type of loss. Where property is to be insured, the person purchasing the insurance must have an *insurable interest* in the property. An insurable interest must be both lawful and substantial where the insurance is against possible liability (like tort liability); the possibility of liability is the basis of the insurable interest. Where insurance is of a person, either a close relationship or a substantial economic interest is necessary for the existence of an insurable interest. A person who insures another is called an *underwriter*.

Is there a situation where the underwriter does not need an insurable interest? Explain.

— — — — — — — — — — — —

The underwriter needs no insurable interest—it is the insurance company. The person buying the insurance is the one who needs the insurable interest.

CHAPTER 3 SELF-TEST

The following questions will help you test your understanding of the terms and concepts in this chapter. Check your answers with those that follow the test. If they do not agree, you may want to review the appropriate part of the chapter.

1. What is the difference between compensatory and punitive damages?

2. If Mark were in the park practicing golf, and accidentally hit Tom with the ball, would he have committed a battery? Explain.

3. If Bob deliberately hit Concetta with a snowball, does that constitute a battery? Explain.

4. Dick and Jane bump fenders at 4th Street. It is Dick's fault. While they are stopped, Jane's car is demolished by a meteor. If it had not been for the accident, she would have been on 14th Street by the time of the accident. Is Dick responsible for the damage? Explain.

5. Stinky is riding his bicycle blindfolded, with no hands. Louis is riding toward the same intersection, and has the right of way. He sees Stinky coming, but realizes that Stinky has a stop sign. Who is liable when they collide? Explain.

6. Does all tort liability depend on intention or negligence? Explain.

7. What is the difference between slander and libel?

8. Which of the following is (are) a possible basis for an insurable interest?

    _____ ownership of property
    _____ acquaintance with the insured person
    _____ the possibility of liability
    _____ a contract of indemnity

ANSWERS

1. Compensatory damages reimburse the plaintiff for actual losses; punitive damages are in excess of any actual harm and are awarded only in certain cases.

2. No. Battery is an intentional tort, and Mark did not intend to hit Tom.

3. Maybe. (There might be consent. For example, Concetta might have started a snowball fight with Bob.)

4. No. The accident was not the proximate cause of the damage. Dick is responsible only for the damage he caused; the rest is too remote.

5. It depends on the rule in their jurisdiction. Louis had the last clear chance and was probably also slightly negligent in not stopping. Stinky was obviously negligent.

6. No. Strict liability, for example, does not.

7. Libel is written; slander is spoken.

8. Ownership of property and the possibility of liability are both possible bases. Mere acquaintance is not enough. A close relationship or a financial interest is necessary.

CHAPTER FOUR

Contracts

When two parties make promises to one another, the promises would be of little value if they could not be enforced in some way. The law of contracts, discussed in this chapter, governs such enforcement.

1. Most simply, a *contract* is an agreement, either written or oral, to do or not do some act. It must not violate any law, and it must be supported by *consideration.* Consideration may be almost any kind of legal *detriment* (harm or loss) that is bargained in exchange for the promise or agreement in the contract. It may be anything from money to another promise, but no contract exists where one of the parties has no obligations whatsoever. The consideration may only be *nominal* (as little as $1, for example), but there must be some consideration or *quid pro quo.* The first element in the formation of a contract is an *offer*, or a proposal of terms. Once there has been an *acceptance* of the offer, a contract has been formed. Once there is a written agreement, no *extrinsic* outside evidence can be used to modify the writing (oral evidence, for example). This rule is called the *parol evidence* rule: the contract must be interpreted strictly on its *face* (within the *four corners*), without any oral (parol) evidence.

    (a) What is extrinsic evidence?

    (b) Which of the following could be consideration for the formation of a contract?

_____ (1) promise not to rob the other party's house
_____ (2) promise not to buy all the milk at the local super-
market
_____ (3) payment of $1
_____ (4) promise not to join the army
_____ (5) promise to repay a debt of $5,000

_ _ _ _ _ _ _ _ _ _ _ _

(a) Extrinsic means from an outside or foreign source—in this
case, from a source other than the written agreement.

(b) 2, 3, and 4. Since robbery is an illegal act, the first cannot
be consideration, and the last is already an existing obligation
(not a new legal detriment).

2. Even when people reach agreement and sign what purports to be a
contract, it is not necessarily valid. For example, if one party is an *infant*
at the time the agreement is made, it cannot be enforced against him. An
infant, or *minor*, is usually any person who has not reached his
eighteenth birthday. Infancy is not the only *impediment* or *incapacity*
that will prevent enforcement of a contract. An adjudication of mental
incompetency has the same effect.
  Even if the parties do have the *capacity* to make a contract, a contract
to do something illegal, like robbing a bank, cannot be enforced. When
the inducement for a contract is mistake, *fraud* (deceit), or *duress*
(wrongful compulsion), it may also be invalidated. Furthermore, a contract that is so one-sided as to be *unconscionable* will generally not be
upheld. Such an agreement is called an *adhesion contract.*

(a) Roger, nineteen years old, needs a refrigerator, but he cannot pay cash for it. He buys it from Acme Appliances on a
financing plan under which he ends up having to pay eight times
the cash price of the refrigerator over a three-year period. Is the
contract valid? Explain.

(b) Humpthistle, an eccentric man who visits his psychiatrist
three times a week, contracts to buy a $3 million schooner as
a decoration for his backyard in Nebraska. When his wife hears
this, she is furious, and wants to prevent it. Is the contract valid?
Explain.

_ _ _ _ _ _ _ _ _ _ _ _

(a) Probably not. Roger is not a minor, but the terms of the contract are so unfair that it will probably be held to be unconscionable and not enforced.

(b) Yes. Humpthistle is not an adjudicated incompetent, and nothing else seems wrong with the deal. Courts cannot supervise the spending of every eccentric person, and it takes more than eccentricity to support an adjudication of incompetence.

3. When one party fails to perform his part of a contract, the other party may be entitled to some *remedy*. If the *damages* were *foreseeable* at the time of the agreement, they may be recovered when the contract is *breached*, although the nonbreaching party has the duty to try to *mitigate* damages, and can only recover for those he could not avoid. Where one party has made some payment and the other party then fails to perform his obligations, the remedy may be a *restitution*, or repayment of what has been wrongly taken.

When there is a dispute about rights under a contract, the parties will try to reach an *accord*, or agreement, and eventually a satisfaction, or discharge of the obligations involved. When a contract is *rescinded* or otherwise terminated before it is fully executed, a party who has partially performed his obligation may be compensated in *quantum meruit* and paid the actual value of his services so far.

(a) If Josh is wrongfully fired from his job, and he is out of work for a year, what might limit his right to recover damages from his former employer?

_____ quantum meruit
_____ the breach of his contract of employment
_____ restitution
_____ the foreseeability of the damages
_____ the duty to mitigate

(b) When does one have the right to breach a contract? Explain.

_ _ _ _ _ _ _ _ _ _ _ _

(a) The duty to mitigate. He can only recover if he was actually unable to find another comparable job.

(b) This is rather a trick question. One always has the right to breach a contract as long as one is willing to pay the consequences.

4. Many contracts deal simply with the *sale* of some goods. Such agreements are governed by the Uniform Commercial Code (U.C.C.), a set of rules that has been adopted in 49 of the 50 states. (The exception is Louisiana.) The U.C.C. sets out the rights and obligations of the *buyer* and *seller.* Where a sale of goods is involved, the question of *warranties* often comes up. A warranty is a guaranty against defects in the goods being sold. In addition to warranties that are expressly made by the seller, other warranties are sometimes implied. For example, when a *merchant* sells goods, there is the implied warranty that they are *merchantable*, or of *salable* quality, suitable for their ordinary purpose. A merchant can, of course, make a *disclaimer* of all implied warranties simply by indicating that the goods are for sale "as is."

(a) Which of the following potential sellers would be likely to be held to an implied warranty on a used radio?

_____ (1) a private owner who decides to sell
_____ (2) an electronics store
_____ (3) a florist
_____ (4) an automobile dealer

(b) If a merchant sells goods without a written contract, can he be held liable on an implied warranty? Explain.

– – – – – – – – – – – – – –

(a) 2 only. Although 3 and 4 are merchants, they do not deal in radios. The implied warranty usually applies only to a merchant in the field in question.

(b) Yes. Remember, not all contracts are written. As long as there is no disclaimer, the merchant automatically gives an implied warranty of merchantability.

5. Another specific area of contract law is *suretyship.* Very simply, a *surety* is one who undertakes to *guaranty* the *debt* of another. Three people, then, are involved. First, there is the *creditor*, the person to whom the debt is owed; second, there is the original *debtor* (sometimes called the principal), who owes the debt; and finally, there is the surety. Surety agreements are contracts and follow the rules of contracts. They must always, however, be written in order to be enforceable.
   In return for his guaranty of the principal debtor, the surety has

certain rights. If the surety is called upon to pay, he is entitled to be reimbursed. This is called *indemnification.* Further, once he has paid the debt, he is entitled to any rights the creditor had against the original debtor. This is called *subrogation.* The surety, however, does not have to pay first to exercise any of his rights. He has the right of *exoneration;* that is, he can sue to compel the original debtor to make payment to the creditor.

(a) A guaranty of reimbursement is known as

——— suretyship.
——— subrogation.
——— exoneration.
——— indemnification.

(b) An agreement of suretyship

——— is a contract.
——— is unenforceable.
——— always leads to indemnification.
——— must be in writing.

— — — — — — — — — — — — —

(a) Indemnification.

(b) It is a contract and it must be in writing. Indemnification is only relevant if the surety is called upon to pay.

CHAPTER 4 SELF-TEST

The following questions will help you test your understanding of the terms and concepts in this chapter. Check your answers with those that follow the test. If they do not agree, you may want to review the appropriate part of the chapter.

1. Consideration is

    _____ a legal detriment.
    _____ *quid pro quo.*
    _____ given in exchange for a promise.
    _____ a necessary part of a contract.

2. Which of the following would not make a contract invalid?

    _____ minority of one party
    _____ the fact that it is a bad deal for one party
    _____ mental incapacity of one party
    _____ the fact that one party was tricked into signing

3. What is parol evidence?

4. What is restitution?

5. To be merchantable, goods must be

    _____ sold by a merchant.
    _____ in perfect condition.
    _____ disclaimed.
    _____ suitable for ordinary use.

6. What do we call the relationship between two parties, whereby one agrees to undertake the debts of the other?

7. The person to whom a debt is owed is called a

    _____ creditor.
    _____ debtor.
    _____ surety.
    _____ indemnity.

ANSWERS

1. Consideration is all these things.

2. The fact that it is a bad deal for one party. A bad deal will not invalidate a contract; it would have to be so bad as to be unconscionable.

3. Parol evidence is extrinsic evidence. It cannot be used to explain what a contract means; the contract must be interpreted strictly on its face.

4. Restitution is repayment. In contract law it is necessary to make restitution when one has taken advantage of another's performance under a contract without performing one's own part of the bargain.

5. Suitable for ordinary use. That is what the word means. (Although anything sold by a merchant must be merchantable, the reverse is not necessarily true; a nonmerchant, as well, can sell merchantable goods.)

6. Suretyship.

7. Creditor.

CHAPTER FIVE

Property

Since the beginning of civilization, property has been an important concept, and one which has caused many disputes. Over the years, a complex set of rules of ownership has evolved. This chapter deals with the laws of property.

1. *Property* is anything that can be owned. We will talk first about *personal property* (or *chattels*), which includes all movable property (as opposed to land). Chattels may be *tangible* (subject to physical possession) or *intangible* (having no physical substance, like a bank account). Chattels are transferred primarily by sale or by *gift*, although there are several other less important, more technical ways for them to change hands. When a gift is given, the person giving it is called the *donor* and the recipient is the *donee*.

   Ownership and *possession* are two different concepts, but the old adage that "possession is nine points of the law" (whatever it means) may well be valid. In the case of lost property, for example, the finder is entitled to retain possession against anybody except the true owner, unless it was found on private property, in which case the owner of the land has a superior right to that of the finder.

   If Maron finds a toy tape recorder that has been lost by Mark, her right of possession is superior to that of

   _____ Mark.
   _____ Millicent, who originally gave the toy to Mark as a gift.
   _____ Melvin, who saw it first but went home to get a wheelbarrow to transport it.
   _____ anybody except Mark.

_ _ _ _ _ _ _ _ _ _ _ _

Millicent and Melvin. We cannot include the fourth choice, because, if the toy was found on private property, the owner of the land would have a right superior to that of anyone but Mark.

2. *Real property* is land and any other immovable property (such as buildings). A possessory interest in real property is called an *estate*. There are several different types of estates, distinguishable from each other by their potential durations. The most extensive is the estate in *fee simple*, which has the potential to endure forever. A *fee tail* has the same potential, but on the death of the owner, it can only be passed on to his children. Should an owner fail to have children, the estate would be lost. The fee tail has been abolished in almost every state. An estate that ends on the death of a particular person is called a *life estate*. The measuring life may be that of the holder of the estate or of a third person. Another estate, which we will discuss in frame 5, is the *leasehold*, the estate of a person who occupies real property by *lease*.

   (a) What is an estate?

   (b) Which of the following estates have the potential to endure forever?

     _____ fee simple
     _____ fee tail
     _____ life estate
     _____ leasehold

- - - - - - - - - - -

   (a) An estate is a possessory interest in real property.

   (b) Fee simple and fee tail, although a fee tail also has the potential to end if one of its holders has no children.

3. Not all interests in land imply immediate possession. A *future interest* is a current right to some possible future possession. The *grantor*, or person transferring an estate, may retain some interest for himself. The creation of a life estate is an example; at the end of the life estate, the grantor has a *reversion*, and the estate returns to him. There are other future interests that raise the possibility of the estate returning to the grantor, but only under certain conditions. The grantor, however, is not the only one who can have a future interest. Returning to the example of the life estate, the grantor can provide that at the end of the life

estate the property passes to a third party. This third party is said to have a *remainder.*

Creation of a life estate necessitates the creation of

_____ a remainder.
_____ a reversion.
_____ some future interest.
_____ none of the above.

— — — — — — — — — — — —

Some future interest (either a reversion or a remainder). In fact, if a life estate is created and no provision at all is made for what happens after the estate ends, a reversion is created automatically by operation of law. Otherwise, the estate would be left with no owner.

4. The most obvious way to obtain *title* (full ownership) to land is by buying it from someone who owns it in fee simple. The transfer, or *grant*, is accomplished in a signed *deed*, which must contain a *habendum* clause, a clause that gives a complete description of the property being transferred. A *recording act* generally requires the *recording* (official notation) of all deeds, thereby making it possible to trace the *chain of title* for a given *parcel* or *tract* of land.
   A second way to obtain title to land is by *prescription*, or *adverse possession.* A person who is not the lawful owner of land can gain title to it by holding it openly and notoriously for a length of time pre-scribed by a *statute of limitations.* Once this time has run out on the original owner's right to eject the adverse possessor, the original owner has no further rights, and the adverse possessor becomes the owner in fee simple, with a new title.

   (a) What is a habendum clause?

   (b) Through which of the following methods can title in fee simple be obtained?

   _____ grant
   _____ sale
   _____ prescription
   _____ adverse possession
   _____ recording

   — — — — — — — — — — — —

(a) A habendum clause is a clause in a deed which gives a complete description of the property being transferred.

(b) All except recording, which is a way to make a public record of a transfer of property, not a way to actually transfer property.

5. It is, of course, possible to occupy real property legally without being the owner. A *leasehold* estate exists when one person *rents* property from another. A *landlord–tenant* relationship is thus created. The *tenancy* may be for any length of time specified in the lease, or it may be at the will of both parties, terminable by either the *lessor* (landlord) or the *lessee* (tenant) at any time. Landlord–tenant law has become a tremendously complex field. Each party has rights and duties: for example, the landlord must deliver the premises in habitable condition and protect the tenant's quiet enjoyment; the tenant must pay rent.

Several variations in the structure of relationships exist in multiple dwellings. In a *cooperative*, the building is owned by a corporation in which the people who occupy it buy shares. They are thus both landlords and tenants at the same time. In a *condominium*, each tenant is sole owner of his own apartment, and all are joint owners of the common areas.

(a) An occupant has sole ownership of his own apartment in

_____ a cooperative only.
_____ a cooperative and a condominium.
_____ leasehold only.
_____ a condominium only.
_____ a leasehold and a condominium.

(b) Who is the landlord in a cooperative? In a condominium? Explain.

_ _ _ _ _ _ _ _ _ _ _ _

(a) In a condominium only. In a cooperative, the entire building is owned by the corporation, which is in turn owned by all the tenants.

(b) In a cooperative the tenants themselves, through their corporation, are the landlord. A condominium is usually directly owned by the occupants. In neither case is there actually a landlord.

6. A person can have certain rights on land owned by another. One example we have just examined is the case of a tenant. Another is an *easement,* the right of one person to use the land of another for a specified purpose. The best example is a right of way over a neighbor's land. Easements may be acquired in the same ways as title to land: by grant, sale, and prescription. To acquire an easement (as opposed to title) by prescription, one must use the land (rather than hold it) for the statutory period.

    A *covenant* is a promise contained in a deed, in which one party agrees to do or not to do something. Where an easement grants certain rights to an outside party, a covenant generally restricts the owner's right to use his land. Covenants generally *run with the land;* that is, they bind all future as well as present owners.

    The government also may place certain restrictions on the use of land. For example, *zoning* can restrict the use of property by making certain uses illegal in certain zones. Thus, commercial property may be separated from residential property. The government also has the power of *eminent domain*, by which it can take property for public use, as long as it compensates the owner. The exercise of eminent domain is called *condemnation.*

    (a) Bobby has been walking across Doug's property on a regular basis for the past 20 years, because it saves him about 25 minutes in getting to the road. Now Doug wants to put up a fence to keep Bobby off. Can Bobby stop him? Explain.

    (b) What is the government's taking of property for public use called?

    (c) A covenant that binds future owners of property is said to

    _____ .

    _ _ _ _ _ _ _ _ _ _ _ _

    (a) Bobby may have acquired an easement by prescription.

    (b) Condemnation. The power to take the property is called eminent domain.

    (c) run with the land

CHAPTER 5 SELF-TEST

The following questions will help you test your understanding of the terms and concepts in this chapter. Check your answers with those that follow the test. If they do not agree, you may want to review the appropriate part of the chapter.

1. Which of the following is (are) intangible property?

    _____ real property
    _____ a debt
    _____ a family pet
    _____ a bank account

2. If Tom is walking across Perriwinkle Acre and finds a guitar, list the following people in order of the strength of their claims to the guitar.

    _____ (a) Tom
    _____ (b) the rightful owner
    _____ (c) the owner of Perriwinkle Acre
    _____ (d) the owner of the store where the guitar was originally purchased

3. When does a life estate terminate?

4. (a) Which of the following are future interests? _____

    (b) Which in the grantor? _____

    (1) life estate
    (2) reversion
    (3) remainder
    (4) leasehold
    (5) easement

5. What is prescription?

6. When does a leasehold estate terminate?

7. Which of the following apply to easement? _____

    Which to covenants? _____

(a) They can be created by grant.
(b) They are contained in deeds.
(c) It is a promise.
(d) It can be sold.
(e) It can be acquired by prescription.

8. What is the meaning of "running with the land"?

9. What is eminent domain?

ANSWERS

1. A debt and a bank account.

2. b, c, a, d.

3. A life estate terminates at the death of the person who is the measuring life. It need not be the owner of the estate.

4. (a) Reversion and remainder are future interests.
   (b) Reversion is a future interest in the grantor.

5. Prescription is the gaining of title to land by adverse possession: openly and notoriously holding land that does not belong to one until the statute of limitations has run out on the original owner's suit to evict the adverse possessor.

6. A leasehold estate terminates at the end of the lease, or, in the case of a tenancy at will, at the will of either party.

7. Easements (a, d, and e) are created in all of the same ways that title to land is acquired; covenants (b and c) are promises contained in deeds.

8. A covenant that runs with the land binds all future owners of the land.

9. Eminent domain, or condemnation, is the right of the government to take private property for public use, compensating the owner for the value of the property taken.

CHAPTER SIX

Business Affiliations and Commercial Transactions

Modern society depends for its very existence on the ability of its members to do business with each other. In this chapter we will discuss some of the laws of the business world.

1. People are not always able to handle personally all of their own business. Sometimes one person, the *principal*, will authorize an *agent* to represent him. Anyone who has the capacity to make a contract can appoint an agent; anyone at all can be an agent for another. The agent's power to act for his principal is called *authority*. The authority may be *actual*, either expressed or implied by the principal to the agent, or it may be *apparent*, where the principal has done something to give third parties the impression that authority exists where it does not. If the agent is acting within his authority, he has the power to act for and bind the principal. Furthermore, a principal may be held liable for torts committed by his agent within the scope of the agency.

   (a) An agent can bind a principal if he has

   ———— actual authority.
   ———— apparent authority.
   ———— no authority at all.

   (b) Apparent authority depends on

   ———— the intent of the principal.
   ———— the belief of the principal.
   ———— the belief of the agent.
   ———— the belief of a third party.

(c) What qualification must a principal have that is unnecessary for an agent?

_ _ _ _ _ _ _ _ _ _ _ _ _

(a) Actual authority or apparent authority. There must be some authority.

(b) The belief of a third party. Apparent authority exists when the principal somehow gives a third party the impression that the agent has the authority to act on the principal's behalf.

(c) Capacity to make a contract.

2. Sometimes, people who want to do business together form a *partnership*, which is an association of two or more competent persons who are co-owners of a business for profit. In effect, each *partner* is the agent of each other partner with regard to the affairs of the partnership. A partnership is not itself a legal entity, so the partners themselves are personally liable for any debts of the partnership. The partnership may be dissolved at any time by any of the partners. The *dissolution* of the partnership does not necessarily mean that the business is ended; it simply means that the relationship has changed somehow. A partner who pulls out of the partnership may be liable for breach of contract.

What happens if a partnership owes more money than it has?

_ _ _ _ _ _ _ _ _ _ _ _ _

The partners themselves are personally liable.

3. There is, however, a business entity that allows the owners to avoid personal liability: the *corporation*. A corporation is an artificial person, which is created by law for business purposes. It can own property, enter into contracts, and remain in existence perpetually. A corporation is owned through the purchase of corporate *stock*, and the *shareholders*, or owners, cannot be held personally liable for the debts of the corporation; liability is limited to the extent of the corporate *assets* (except in cases of fraud). The shareholders also do not have direct control over the operation of the corporation; they adopt a set of *by-laws* to govern the running of the corporation and they elect a board of directors to manage the business. The directors are usually elected annually.

The *officers* of a corporation are generally elected by the board of directors, although the shareholders may reserve the right for themselves. The officers act as agents of the corporation; for example, the president usually has the authority to make contracts, the treasurer may be authorized to act with respect to the finances of the corporation.

Identify which of the following statements describe more accurately a corporation and which a partnership:

_____ (1) Owners are personally liable for debts of the business.
_____ (2) It is an artificial person.
_____ (3) It exists perpetually.
_____ (4) Owners have direct control over its operation.

- - - - - - - - - - - - - -

(1) partnership
(2) corporation
(3) corporation
(4) partnership

4. When the corporation is formed, shares may be given for money, services, or property, but not on credit for any future obligations. The original value of the shares is fixed by the board of directors; if a value is written on the shares, it is called *par value.* The stated *capital* of the corporation is the total par value of the shares sold or, if the shares have no par value, the value of what is received in exchange for them. Of course, the stated capital may be only a fraction of the company's total capital, or *net* worth (the total that remains after expenses). The shares themselves are represented by *certificates.* From time to time, if the corporation is doing well, it may pay a *dividend* to the shareholders. The dividend may be in cash or in more shares of stock. On dissolution of the corporation, its assets are distributed among the shareholders.

(a) Which contributes more to the total capital of a corporation, the sale of a $10 par value share for $15 or the sale of a no-par-value share for $15? Explain.

(b) Could corporation shares be given on formation in exchange for a promise to work for the corporation for the next five years? Explain.

- - - - - - - - - - - - -

(a) They have the same effect on total capital. However, the second sale adds $15 to the *stated* capital, whereas the first adds only $10.

(b) No. The value given in exchange for shares must be current. Future employment is not a satisfactory substitute for current value.

5. Obviously, the business world would be a difficult place if all transactions had to be made in cash. Fortunately, *commercial paper (negotiable instruments)* exists. A negotiable instrument is a signed paper that absolutely promises to pay a specific sum of money at a specific time or on *demand* either to the *bearer* or to the order of a specific person. A *bill of exchange* or a *draft* is a written order from one person, the *drawer*, to another, the *drawee*, to pay money to a third person, the *payee*. A *check* is an example of a draft. A *promissory note* is a written, unconditional promise to pay a specific amount of money at a specific time.

(a) Which of the following necessarily contain(s) an order to

pay? _____

    (1) a negotiable instrument
    (2) a bill of exchange
    (3) a draft
    (4) a check
    (5) a promissory note

(b) Which of the following is (are) not necessary in order for an

instrument to be negotiable? _____

    (1) the signature of the drawer
    (2) the signature of the drawee
    (3) that it specify a sum of money
    (4) the signature of the payee
    (5) that there be some time certainty
    (6) an unconditional promise

— — — — — — — — — — — —

(a) 2, 3, and 4. A promissory note (a form of negotiable instrument) contains a promise, but no order.

(b) 2 and 4. Only the drawer need sign, but the instrument must be an unconditional promise to pay a specific sum of money at a specific time (or on demand). The payee may be required to sign at the time of negotiation, but the instrument is negotiable when it is drawn.

6. The *holder* (possessor) of a negotiable instrument must, of course, have a way to *negotiate*, or transfer, the instrument to another party. If the instrument is payable to the bearer, this can be done simply by *delivery* of the instrument. If, on the other hand, it is payable to the order of some person, that person must also sign his name on the back of the instrument. That process is called *indorsement.* When the drawee bank guarantees payment of a check, that check is said to be *certified*, and the bank, rather than the drawer, is then primarily liable.

   (a) Who is a holder of an instrument?

   (b) What kind of instrument requires an indorsement for negotiation?

   _ _ _ _ _ _ _ _ _ _ _ _ _

   (a) Anyone in possession of an instrument is a holder.

   (b) An instrument payable to the order of someone requires indorsement; bearer paper requires only delivery.

7. Sometimes when a creditor loans money or otherwise extends credit to a debtor, he wants the debt to be secured with some kind of interest in property, a security interest. When an obligation is so secured, it is called a *secured transaction.* For the security interest to be created, the debtor must sign an agreement. Creation of a security interest is also known as *attachment.* Attachment of the interest is enough to give the creditor's claim priority over the claims of most other creditors, but in order to get the maximum protection it is necessary to *perfect* the security interest. This is usually done by *filing* or by taking possession of the property in question.

Another word used to describe the creation of a security interest
is

_____ perfection.
_____ filing.
_____ transaction.
_____ attachment.

— — — — — — — — — — — —

Attachment.

CHAPTER 6 SELF-TEST

The following questions will help you test your understanding of the terms and concepts in this chapter. Check your answers with those that follow the test. If they do not agree, you may want to review the appropriate part of the chapter.

1. Who can be an agent for another? Who can be a principal?

2. When does an agent have actual authority? Apparent authority?

3. To what extent are partners obligated to remain in the partnership? Explain.

4. To what extent are the owners liable for the debts of the partnership? Of a corporation?

5. Who is responsible for managing a corporation?

   _____ the shareholders
   _____ the directors
   _____ the officers

6. Which of the following could not be accepted in exchange for shares of stock in a new corporation?

   _____ money
   _____ property
   _____ services
   _____ promise of future services

7. A personal check is a type of

   _____ negotiable instrument.
   _____ draft.
   _____ bill of exchange.
   _____ all of the above.

8. Could a note that promised to pay "the fair value of 100 pounds of clay on May 31, 1985" be a valid negotiable instrument? Explain.

9. What steps are necessary to negotiate an instrument made payable to the order of a particular person?

10. Filing a security agreement is one way of

_____ perfecting it.
_____ attachment.
_____ securing it.
_____ incorporation.

ANSWERS

1. Anyone can be an agent; anyone with contractual capacity can appoint an agent.

2. An agent has actual authority when it has been communicated to him by his principal; he has apparent authority when the principal has indicated to a third party that the agent is authorized.

3. A partner is always free to withdraw from the partnership—the only sanction is a possible suit for breach of contract.

4. The owners of a partnership have personal liability for all the debts of the partnership; the liability of the owners of a corporation is limited to the corporate assets.

5. The directors.

6. Promise of future services.

7. Negotiable instrument.

8. No. It does not promise payment of a *specific* sum of money. It is impossible to say what the clay will be worth on May 31, 1985.

9. Indorsement and delivery. In the case of bearer paper, only delivery is necessary.

10. Perfecting it. Taking possession of the property is another.

CHAPTER SEVEN

Wills, Trusts, and Family Law

The law touches our domestic lives and even our deaths. This chapter deals with several instances of both, including wills, trusts, and family law.

1. When a person dies, the total of all the property he leaves behind makes up his *estate*. The distribution of the dead person's estate is governed by a fairly complex set of rules. If the dead person, or *decedent*, did not leave a valid *will*, he is said to have died *intestate*. In that case, his estate is *inherited* by his *heirs*, who are generally his closest living relatives. It is significant to note that a man's heirs are not determined until his death—the living have no heirs. Only the relatives who survive the decedent, therefore, become his heirs. If a decedent leaves neither a will nor any heirs, his estate will *escheat* to the state. In other words, when there is no way to determine a legal owner of a decedent's property, it will pass to the state.

    (a) A person has no heirs when he

    _____ dies intestate.
    _____ leaves a will.
    _____ is alive.
    _____ has no estate.

    (b) A decedent's property will escheat to the state if the decedent

    _____ has no heirs.
    _____ has no estate.
    _____ dies intestate.
    _____ leaves a will.

- - - - - - - - - - - - -

(a) The only thing on this list that prevents a person from having heirs is being alive. Whether or not he leaves a will or any estate makes no difference.

(b) Has no heirs and dies intestate (without a will).

2. For a writing to be a valid will, it must meet certain formal requirements. First the person executing the will must have *testamentary* capacity at the time the will is executed. That is, the *testator* must be at least a certain age (usually eighteen or twenty-one) and must not be a mental incompetent (the standard of mental competency here is much lower than the standard required for contractual capacity). Second, the will itself must meet certain statutory formalities. The will must be *subscribed* (signed at the end) by the testator and by at least two witnesses who are aware that they are witnessing a will. *Nuncupative* (oral) wills and *holographs* (completely handwritten wills) that are not executed with all the proper formalities are recognized in some states. Many states, however, require full formalities for a holograph will and all require that it be subscribed.

(a) Does a holograph have to be witnessed? Explain.

(b) Billy Budapest lacks the mental competency to make a contract. However, he makes a will leaving his entire fortune to Professor Lopes. Can the will be valid? Explain.

(c) Does a nuncupative will have to be subscribed? Explain.

– – – – – – – – – – – –

(a) Some states will recognize an unwitnessed holograph (handwritten will), at least in some situations, but many states require full formalities for a holograph.

(b) The will may be valid if Mr. Budapest has testamentary capacity, which is judged by a less strict standard than is contractual capacity. A person not considered competent to make a contract may still be able to write a valid will.

(c) No. It would be difficult to sign an oral will.

3. The fact that a person writes a valid will does not mean that he cannot change his mind; wills can be *revoked* (canceled) or revised. Of course, the execution of a new will acts to revoke the old will. It is also possible to supplement or change an existing will by writing the changes in what must be a fully executed testamentary instrument. Such a supplement is called a *codicil.* A will can also be revoked when the testator destroys it or by operation of law (e.g., when the testator marries after writing his will, the law will automatically protect the new spouse). *Ademption* of a *bequest* or *legacy* is also possible; ademption occurs when the testator, while he is still alive, gives the item to the *beneficiary* (the intended recipient), thus making the provision in the will academic.

    On the death of the testator, the provisions of his will are carried out by the *executor*, if the testator has designated one in his will, or by a court-appointed *administrator.*

    (a) What is ademption?

    (b) What is the difference between an executor and an adminis-trator?

    — — — — — — — — — — —

    (a) Ademption is the satisfaction of a legacy (bequest) after the writing of a will, by some act of the testator.

    (b) An executor is named by the testator (in his will); an administrator is appointed by a court.

4. A *trust* is a *fiduciary* relationship in which one party, the *trustee,* holds some assets for the benefit of another, the beneficiary, also known as the *cestui que trust.* The person who creates a trust is called the *settlor* (or *trustor*). The settlor's intention to create a trust must be clear; *precatory* (requesting) language such as "I would like" will not suffice. There must be an explicit command. Trusts can be created by will or during the settlor's lifetime (*inter vivos*). The creation of a trust generally must follow certain formal requisites. The *Totten trust,* however, bypasses some of the requirements. It is a bank account deposited by one person in trust for another. It is revocable at the will of the depositor, but passes automatically on his death to the beneficiary.

(a) The cestui que trust is the

_____ beneficiary.

_____ settlor.

_____ trustee.

_____ trustor.

(b) When does a Totten trust pass to the beneficiary?

_ _ _ _ _ _ _ _ _ _ _ _ _

(a) Beneficiary.

(b) A Totten trust passes to the beneficiary on the death of the depositor.

5. Charitable trusts are protected by a special set of rules. To qualify, a trust must be for a charitable purpose. When a charitable gift cannot be carried out exactly as specified, the doctrine of *cy pres* applies, allowing courts to carry it out as closely to the intent of the settlor as possible. Cy pres is applied only when consistent with the apparent intention of the settlor.

Another special trust is the *spendthrift trust.* Its provisions prevent the premature dissipation of the assets of the trust by forbidding prospective transfer of the income from the fund. A settlor must generally specify that he wants to create a spendthrift trust, but in some states it is automatic.

What protection does a spendthrift trust afford?

_ _ _ _ _ _ _ _ _ _ _ _ _

It protects the beneficiary against the premature dissipation of the assets of the trust.

6. Family law deals to a large extent with *matrimonial* situations. Any agreements entered into between the parties before the marriage are termed *antenuptial.* The marriage itself is usually accomplished by ceremony, but some states recognize *common law marriages* when the parties live together as husband and wife for a certain amount of time. Obviously, married people have certain duties and obligations to each other.

When one party fails to meet those obligations, or if there is another valid reason, the marriage may be ended. Some marriages are *void* (e.g., an *incestuous* or *bigamous* marriage). Such marriages are a nullity and will be declared so automatically by a court. Others are *voidable* through a process called *annulment* (e.g., when one party is under the legal age). A marriage can also be ended by *divorce*, or by court order. The various states require different grounds for divorce, ranging from simple incompatibility to *abandonment* and *adultery*.

(a) How does annulment differ from divorce?

(b) How does a common law marriage differ from a ceremonial marriage?

– – – – – – – – – – – –

(a) When a marriage is ended by annulment, it is voided; it is as if it never happened. A divorce, though, ends a valid marriage by court order, and the record remains.

(b) They differ in the way they are created; a common law marriage, where recognized, involves only living together as husband and wife for a certain length of time, rather than involving a ceremony.

CHAPTER 7 SELF-TEST

The following questions will help you test your understanding of the terms and concepts in this chapter. Check your answers with those that follow the test. If they do not agree, you may want to review the appropriate part of the chapter.

1. When does property escheat to the state?

2. What is a nuncupative will?

3. Does a holograph have to be subscribed?

4. How do the formal requirements for a valid codicil differ from those of a will?

5. The trustee holds money or property for the benefit of the

   _____ beneficiary.
   _____ settlor.
   _____ trustor.
   _____ cestui que trust.

6. The subject of a Totten trust is

   _____ precatory.
   _____ inter vivos.
   _____ a bank account.
   _____ real property.

7. What is the name of the doctrine that allows modification of a charitable trust in accordance with the intent of the settlor? _____

8. A marriage would be void if it were

   _____ incestuous.
   _____ ended in divorce.
   _____ entered into by a minor.
   _____ bigamous.

ANSWERS

1. Property escheats to the state when a person dies intestate leaving no heirs.

2. A nuncupative will is an oral will.

3. Yes. All written wills have to be subscribed (signed at the end). Some states recognize holographs (completely handwritten wills) without some of the formal requirements that are usually necessary for wills.

4. Not at all; a codicil that is also a testamentary instrument is subject to the same requirements as a will.

5. Beneficiary and cestui que trust. They are synonymous.

6. A bank account. In fact, it is sometimes called a bank account trust.

7. The doctrine of cy pres.

8. Incestuous and bigamous. The marriage of a minor might be voidable in some situations, but it is not automatically void.

CHAPTER EIGHT

Criminal Law and Procedure

In some laws society is felt to have such a strong interest that breaking these rules may subject a person to punishment. In this chapter we will discuss the types of behavior proscribed by the criminal law and the procedures used in implementing the law.

1. The subject of criminal law deals primarily with the definition and classification of criminal *offenses*. Offenses are violations of what is called the *penal law* (the law relating to crimes and their punishments), although traffic *infractions*, which we will not deal with here, are considered offenses and are usually handled separately. Generally, an offense is any conduct which, if discovered, can subject the person engaging in it to some penal sanctions, such as being *incarcerated* (imprisoned) or being forced to pay a *fine*.

     Offenses can be divided into *crimes* and violations, crimes being further divided into *felonies* and *misdemeanors*. Felonies are the more serious crimes, usually entailing prison sentences of more than a year. Misdemeanors are less serious and generally carry sentences of less than a year. Violations are far less serious; the maximum sentence for a violation is usually only a couple of weeks. Felonies and misdemeanors are often graded, class A felonies being the most serious crimes, class B felonies next, and so on.

     (a) Name the four classifications of offenses.

(b) Which three offenses are covered by the penal law?

_ _ _ _ _ _ _ _ _ _ _ _

(a) Felonies, misdemeanors, violations, traffic infractions.

(b) Felonies, misdemeanors, violations.

2. For a crime to take place, there must be both a forbidden act and an accompanying mental state. The forbidden act, or *actus reus*, may be either a positive criminal act or, in certain circumstances, a failure to act when the law would require some action. In order for the act to constitute a crime, the accompanying mental state must be *culpable.* This guilty state of mind is called *mens rea*, and most modern codes recognize four kinds of culpability: purpose (or intent), knowledge, recklessness, and negligence.

For example, at *common law*, *murder* was an unlawful killing committed with *malice aforethought.* Under most modern statutes murder is intentional and deliberate killing, although the issue of *premeditation* (planning) may determine the degree of murder charged.

(a) What two elements are needed to constitute a crime?

(b) What are the four recognized culpable states of mind?

_ _ _ _ _ _ _ _ _ _ _ _

(a) *Actus reus* (forbidden act), *mens rea* (culpable state of mind).

(b) Purpose (intent), knowledge, recklessness, negligence.

3. In attempting to classify offenses, the first thing to consider is whether the offense is against a person or against property. The most serious class

of offenses against the person, of course, is *homicide*, the culpable killing by one person of another person. The most serious homicide is *murder*, which is generally an intentional and deliberate killing. Murder may also be committed in a highly *reckless* manner. Many states have laws providing for different degrees of murder, the most common division being that a premeditated murder is first-degree murder and an unpremeditated murder is second-degree murder. In addition, many states have what is called the *felony murder rule*, which states that participants in certain felonies are guilty of murder if any of them causes the death of a non-participant in the crime (providing that the death is caused during the commission of the crime or the immediate flight from the scene). This is true even if the killing was unintentional.

At common law, an intentional killing, or homicide, committed without malice was not a murder, but it could still be considered *manslaughter.* Many states have penal laws providing for several degrees of manslaughter. Manslaughter may be committed voluntarily, involuntarily, or accidentally.

In some states there is also a crime called criminally negligent homicide. It usually refers to deaths caused as a result of the negligent operation of an automobile.

(a) The culpable killing of another person is called

_____ murder.
_____ manslaughter.
_____ felony murder.
_____ homicide.

(b) A and B are committing a robbery together. They leave through separate exits, and on the way out, B kills C, an innocent bystander. A does not know that B killed C. Who is guilty of murder?

(c) Can an accidental killing, in the absence of the commission of a felony, be murder? Why?

_ _ _ _ _ _ _ _ _ _ _ _

(a) Homicide.

(b) Both are. Where it applies, the felony murder rule can make a person guilty of murder even if he does not know that the victim has been hurt.

(c) No, although it might still be a homicide (manslaughter). Murder requires a culpable state of mind.

4. Another punishable offense against the person is assault, which is the causing of physical injury. Assault, like murder and manslaughter, is often graded into several degrees. The degree is usually determined by the type of injury caused, how it was caused (e.g., whether or not a weapon was used), and the state of mind of the person committing the assault. Assaults can be committed intentionally, recklessly, or negligently.

An offense may be punishable even if nobody is hurt. *Reckless endangerment* involves the creation of a risk of death or injury to another person. *Menacing* is an *intentional* placing of another in fear of serious injury, and *harassment* is a catch-all that may include even conduct like cursing, as long as the intent of the actor is somehow to annoy the victim.

(a) Which of the following need not involve actual physical injury?

_____ assault
_____ reckless endangerment
_____ menacing
_____ harassment

(b) Which of the following may *not* require intent?

_____ assault
_____ reckless endangerment
_____ menacing
_____ harassment

_ _ _ _ _ _ _ _ _ _ _ _ _ _

(a) Reckless endangerment, menacing, and harassment.

(b) Assault and reckless endangerment.

5. Certain serious crimes against the person, such as *kidnapping*, are classified separately. Kidnapping involves the movement or restraint of a person against his will. *Abduction* has come to be synonymous with kidnapping, but at common law it referred only to the taking of a child or a wife. *Unlawful imprisonment*, a less serious crime, involves only the restraint of a person against his will.

The major sex crime, of course, is *rape*, which is committed when a male *unlawfully forces* a female to engage in intercourse. Even if force is not used, intercourse with a female younger than a certain age (specified by law in each state) may be *statutory rape.* Other acts widely considered to be crimes are *sodomy* (deviate intercourse), bigamy (being married to two people at the same time), and, in many states, even adultery, which is sexual intercourse between a married person and someone who is not his or her spouse.

Consent of the other party might be a defense to

_____ bigamy.
_____ sodomy.
_____ unlawful imprisonment.
_____ statutory rape.

_ _ _ _ _ _ _ _ _ _ _ _ _

Unlawful imprisonment. Although consent is a defense to rape, statutory rape is a crime even if the minor consents.

6. Offenses against property may involve damaging the property, intruding on it, or somehow stealing it. The most serious of these offenses is *arson*, which consists of an intentional explosion or fire causing damage to some kind of a building. The seriousness of the arson depends on the type of damage, the type of building, who is in the building, and the intention of the actor. Most other intentional or reckless damage to property falls under the heading of *criminal mischief* or its equivalent.

   The offense of intruding on property takes two forms, *burglary* and *criminal trespass* (or its equivalent). Criminal trespass consists simply of entering or remaining unlawfully on the property, with the knowledge that it is unlawful to be there. *Burglary* has the added elements that the property be a building and that the actor intends to commit a crime while in the building. The degree of the burglary depends on the type of building, whether the burglar is armed, whether anyone is hurt, and whether the burglary takes place during the day or night. Generally, nighttime burglaries are more serious. In some jurisdictions, some burglaries committed during daylight hours are called *housebreaking.*

   (a) Which of the following involve damage to property?

_____ arson
_____ burglary
_____ criminal mischief
_____ criminal trespass
_____ housebreaking

(b) Which of the following can only be committed at night?

_____ arson
_____ burglary
_____ criminal mischief
_____ criminal trespass
_____ housebreaking

(c) If Josh enters a building unlawfully at night intending to beat up Idi, but changes his mind and leaves without even touching anything, has he committed a burglary? Explain.

_ _ _ _ _ _ _ _ _ _ _ _ _ _

(a) Arson and criminal mischief.

(b) None of these. (Housebreaking, where it exists, can only be committed during the day.)

(c) Yes. All that is required is the intention to commit any crime while in the building. Josh broke in with the required intention.

7. _Larceny_ is the wrongful taking, or stealing, of property belonging to another. It is a crime that requires that the actor have the intent to deprive the rightful owner of the property taken. It can be accomplished in many ways, including (but not limited to) physical theft of the property involved, _embezzlement_ (the fraudulent taking of money that has been entrusted to the taker), _extortion_ (compelling payment by illegal threats), and writing bad checks. Larceny is graded according to the value of the property stolen: _grand larceny_ involves theft of more than an amount specified by law; _petit larceny_ involves a theft of less than that amount. The _possession_ of stolen property is also a crime. Of course, in order to have the requisite intent for this crime, the possessor would have to believe the property to be stolen.

When the larceny is committed with the use or even the threat of force, it becomes _robbery_. The grading of the robbery depends on whether anyone is actually hurt and what kinds of weapons, if any, are used.

Finally, *forgery* is committed when a document is falsely made or altered with intent to *defraud*. The grading of the crime depends on the type of document involved.

(a) Which of the following would a person necessarily commit in the process of committing a robbery?

_____ larceny
_____ grand larceny
_____ embezzlement
_____ forgery

(b) What is embezzlement?

(c) When Mark moves from one address to another, he changes the address listed on his driver's license. In doing so, he accidentally lists his new address as 322 Main Street instead of 522 Main Street. Has he committed a forgery? Explain.

_ _ _ _ _ _ _ _ _ _ _ _

(a) Larceny.

(b) The fraudulent taking of money that has been entrusted to the taker.

(c) No. He did not intend to defraud any one; he simply made a mistake. Had he entered the wrong address with the intent to defraud some one, however, what he did would have been a forgery.

8. Sometimes even a person who has not actually participated in one of the acts we have listed can have criminal liability. For example, an *accomplice* can be liable for the conduct of the *principal* who actually commits the crime. An accomplice helps a person to commit a crime either before or during the actual commission of the crime. A person who gives aid in any way after the crime has been committed becomes an *accessory* after the fact.

A person can be guilty of *attempt* without being successful in committing a crime. Even the act of agreeing to commit a crime can make those participating guilty of *conspiracy*.

If Eric robs a grocery store and several hours later Bruce tells him that the police are waiting for him at home, Bruce might be guilty of

_____ conspiracy.
_____ being an accomplice.
_____ being an accessory.
_____ no crime at all.

- - - - - - - - - - - -

Being an accessory.

9. Sometimes, even though a person commits an act proscribed by the penal law, he may have no liability because of the existence of some *defense.* Some form of justification, such as self-defense or defense of property, may exist. In some cases, a person may not be legally responsible for his actions, because he is insane or still an *infant*, or because he has been *entrapped* (induced by the police to commit a crime that he would not otherwise have committed).

Which of the following are justification defenses?

_____ entrapment
_____ self-defense
_____ infancy
_____ defense of property

- - - - - - - - - - - -

Self-defense and defense of property.

10. Criminal trials, like most other judicial proceedings, are *adversary proceedings.* Two sides contest the issue, each having an opportunity to be heard. In a criminal trial, the two sides are the *prosecution* and the *defense.* The *prosecutor* represents the People, or the government, and the defense represents the *defendant*, or the person accused of committing the crime. In theory, the prosecutor's job is to see that justice is done; in practice, the prosecutor usually tries as hard as he can to obtain a *conviction* (a verdict of guilty). The defense lawyer's job is to represent his client as vigorously as possible within the rules, and to try to obtain an *acquittal.* A person is always presumed innocent of a crime until the prosecutor can prove him guilty under the rules of evidence beyond a reasonable doubt.

If a defense lawyer believes that his client has committed the crime of which he is accused, what should he do? Why?

— — — — — — — — — — — —

Defend him as well as possible. If the prosecutor cannot prove him guilty, he is not guilty. It is not up to the defense lawyer . to convict his client.

11. Criminal procedure is governed, to a large extent, by the Constitution. The rules deal with the entire process of handling a criminal defendant, before, during, and after trial. Before a case reaches trial, the main area of concern is with evidence and how it is obtained. The *exclusionary rule* dictates that evidence obtained against a defendant as a result of an illegal *search and seizure* cannot be used at trial. What constitutes a valid search and seizure has been the subject of much technical writing. Basically, a search is valid if it is made pursuant to a *search warrant* (a written authorization from a judge or magistrate), when it is con- sented to, when it is made pursuant to a valid *arrest*, or when certain special circumstances exist. An arrest is valid if it is pursuant to a warrant or if the arresting officer had *probable cause* (reasonable cause under the circumstances) for the arrest. When a search is improper, both the evidence seized and any information that results from it are excluded from the judicial process.

(a) The police make an illegal search of Ted's room and find a locker key. At a railroad station, they use the key to open a locker and they find a stolen painting. Can the key be used as evidence at Ted's trial? The painting? Explain.

(b) Can a search ever be valid without a search warrant? Explain.

— — — — — — — — — — — —

(a) Neither one. The police have both as the result of an illegal search.

(b) Yes, if it is consented to or made pursuant to a valid arrest or under special circumstances.

12. Physical evidence is not the only type of damaging evidence that may be excluded when it is improperly obtained. *Confessions* (admissions of guilt), for example, will be suppressed if they are not completely *voluntary*, since the Constitution prohibits compelling a person "to be a witness against himself." Even where a confession is voluntary, it may be suppressed where certain other constitutional rights have been violated. The *Miranda rule* (*Miranda* v. *Arizona*) dictates that a prisoner must be given certain warnings before he can be questioned. He must be told that he has the right to remain silent and to consult a lawyer, and that anything he says may be used as evidence against him.

What is a confession?

— — — — — — — — — — — —

A confession is an admission of guilt of a crime.

13. Once a person has been arrested, he must be *arraigned* without un-necessary delay. At arraignment, the charges are read and the defendant may then be released on *bail* (the payment of money that is forfeited if the defendant fails to appear later). Sometimes the defendant pleads *guilty* or *not guilty* at the arraignment. The criminal proceeding itself is generally begun with the filing of an *accusatory instrument*, either an *indictment* or an *information*. An information is a written accusation generally filed by the prosecutor. An indictment, also a written accusa-tion of a crime, is handed down by a *grand jury*, the jury that decides whether there is enough evidence to warrant a trial.

(a) What happens when a person is arraigned?

(b) What distinguishes an indictment from an information?

— — — — — — — — — — — —

(a) The charges against him are read and his plea is entered.

(b) Both are accusatory instruments, but the indictment must be handed down by a grand jury.

14. In our law, there are some limitations on whether a person can be brought to trial. The most famous, perhaps, is the constitutional prohibi-tion of *double jeopardy*, or trying a person twice for the same offense.

In addition, just as with civil matters, a court may only hear a criminal case if it has jurisdiction, both over the subject matter and the person involved, and the venue must be proper. If a person is to be tried for a crime, the action must be begun in a timely fashion; a *statute of limitations* usually must be observed. The statute will set time limits within which a prosecution must be commenced. Finally, there is a constitutional prohibition of *ex post facto* laws, laws that impose criminal sanctions for an act that was not criminal at the time it was committed.

Name two specific prohibitions against criminal prosecutions found in the Federal Constitution.

— — — — — — — — — — —

The prohibition against double jeopardy; the prohibition of *ex post facto* laws.

15. A person accused of a crime has a right to a *speedy trial*, one free from excessive and unreasonable delays. Once accused, a defendant is entitled to be represented by a lawyer. An *indigent*, or poor person, who cannot afford a lawyer is entitled to have a lawyer appointed by the court to represent him. The Federal Constitution guarantees a defendant the right to a trial by jury and to a public trial. Perhaps the best known trial right is the right not to testify against oneself, granted in the fifth amendment to the Federal Constitution as well as in most state constitutions.

(a) What happens in the case of a defendant who cannot afford a lawyer?

(b) Where is the right not to testify against oneself found?

— — — — — — — — — — —

(a) A lawyer is appointed by the Court.

(b) In the fifth amendment to the Federal Constitution.

16. A defendant is *convicted* when a jury unanimously finds him guilty, or *acquitted* when a jury unanimously declares him not guilty. When the jury is unable to reach a unanimous verdict, it is said to be a *hung jury*, and a *mistrial* is declared. Of course, the defendant is not obligated to

have a jury trial; if he prefers he can be tried in front of the judge without a jury.

After a finding of guilt, the judge generally passes *sentence*, although some states leave the question of punishment up to the jury. Even after he is found guilty, the defendant has the right to *appeal* to a higher court. In addition, the writ of *habeas corpus* exists, as it has since common law days, as a remedy for any unlawful detention. It requires that the prisoner be brought into court so that the legality of the imprisonment can be determined.

In which of the following ways can a defendant be found guilty?

_____ a guilty plea
_____ a finding by a judge
_____ a majority vote of a jury
_____ a writ of habeas corpus

_ _ _ _ _ _ _ _ _ _ _ _ _

A guilty plea or a finding by a judge. A jury verdict must generally be unanimous. Although some states provide for slightly less than unanimity, more than a simple majority is always needed.

CHAPTER 8 SELF-TEST

The following questions will help you test your understanding of the terms and concepts in this chapter. Check your answers with those that follow the test. If they do not agree, you may want to review the appropriate part of the chapter.

1. Which of the following are crimes?

    _____ violations
    _____ felonies
    _____ traffic infractions
    _____ misdemeanors

2. Mens rea is the same thing as

    _____ actus reus.
    _____ guilty mind.
    _____ forbidden act.
    _____ malice.

3. Which of the following includes all the others?

    _____ murder
    _____ criminally negligent homicide
    _____ homicide
    _____ manslaughter

4. If Bob comes across a hunter sleeping in the woods, and steals the wallet which is right next to the hunter's hand, has he committed a robbery? Explain.

5. Which of the following involves physical injury?

    _____ reckless endangerment
    _____ menacing
    _____ harassment
    _____ assault

6. Is it true that a rape can only take place when a male unlawfully forces a female to engage in intercourse? Explain.

7. What crime would a person definitely commit if he threw a bomb into a building (assuming the bomb worked)?

8. For which crime might it make a difference at what time the crime is committed? How?

9. If Fred stops Jim on the street, points a gun at him, and demands his money, but runs away before getting anything because he thinks he hears a police car, Fred has committed

   _____ robbery.
   _____ attempted grand larceny.
   _____ conspiracy.
   _____ attempted robbery.
   _____ no crime at all.

10. Larry attacks Walter with a knife, trying to kill him. Walter pulls out a gun and kills Larry. Is he guilty of a homicide? Explain.

11. Which of the following might make a search legal?

   _____ a warrant
   _____ a valid arrest
   _____ the exclusionary rule
   _____ an ex post facto rule

12. Which of the following are accusatory instruments?

   _____ confession
   _____ indictment
   _____ grand jury
   _____ information

13. What special rights does an indigent defendant have?

14. Who determines what a prisoner's sentence will be?

ANSWERS

1. Felonies and misdemeanors.

2. Guilty mind.

3. Homicide.

4. No. Robbery requires the use of force.

5. Assault

6. No. Having intercourse (even voluntary intercourse) with a girl younger than a certain specified age is statutory rape.

7. Arson. If he planted the bomb, of course, it would also be a burglary.

8. Burglary. Burglary is sometimes more serious if committed at night.

9. Attempted robbery.

10. He might be, but a court might find that he acted in self-defense, in which case his killing of Larry might be justified.

11. A warrant or a valid arrest. The others have nothing to do with valid searches.

12. Indictment and information.

13. None. An indigent has the same rights as any other criminal defendant. Since he cannot afford to exercise them, the state must provide funds to help him.

14. Generally the judge, although in some states it is a function of the jury.

Final Self-Test

The following questions will help you test your understanding of the terms and concepts in this guide. Check your answers with those that follow this test. If they do not agree, you may want to review the chapters and frames given in parentheses.

1. Which of the following applies when the only issue in a case is the status of some real property?

    _____ in personam jurisdiction
    _____ subject matter jurisdiction
    _____ in rem jurisdiction
    _____ quasi in rem jurisdiction

2. What does the summons do?

    _____ invokes the court's jurisdiction
    _____ attaches property
    _____ notifies the defendant
    _____ gives substituted service

3. Which of the following cannot affect the question of federal jurisdiction?

    _____ diversity of citizenship
    _____ venue
    _____ jurisdictional amount
    _____ involvement of a federal question

4. Which of the following pleadings might be filed by a defendant?

_____ answer
_____ reply
_____ complaint
_____ supplemental pleading

5. What is the effect of a long-arm statute?

6. What is the preferred method of serving process?

7. Complete this analogy:

Attachment is to tangibles as _____ is to intangibles.

8. Which of the following are necessary in order for evidence to be admissible?

_____ circumstantiality
_____ relevance
_____ materiality
_____ competence

9. Which of the following are *not* proper grounds to impeach a witness?

_____ bias
_____ interest
_____ inability to perceive
_____ bad reputation for truth

10. Which of the following can be admitted into evidence as exceptions to the rule against hearsay?

_____ an admission
_____ a declaration against interest
_____ declaration of a hostile witness
_____ a dying declaration

11. Which of the following are not intentional torts?

_____ battery
_____ assault
_____ trespass
_____ negligence

12. When may a plaintiff counterclaim? Explain.

13. Compare res judicata and collateral estoppel.

14. Once it has been established that several courts have jurisdiction, the question of which one to initiate the action in is a question of

    _____ .

15. A claim by one defendant against another is a(n) _____ .

16. What is the name given to the plaintiff's presentation of enough evidence to win, assuming that no evidence is presented by the defense?

17. What is the name given to the recognition by a court of certain well-known facts, not in evidence?

18. Compare slander and libel.

19. Which of the following are synonymous with compensatory damages?

    _____ actual damages
    _____ punitive damages
    _____ exemplary damages
    _____ intentional damages

20. Which of the following could be defenses in a tort case?

    _____ res ipsa loquitur
    _____ contributory negligence
    _____ assumption of risk
    _____ last clear chance

21. The parol evidence rule is most closely associated with the subject of

    _____ torts
    _____ contracts
    _____ criminal law
    _____ property

22. Which of the following could render a contract invalid?

      _____ unprofitability
      _____ fraud
      _____ minority of one party
      _____ illegality

23. Can a seller be held responsible for anything which is not covered by an express warranty? Explain.

24. Who has the strongest right to ownership of lost property?

25. Whose life is used to measure a life estate?

26. Compare a cooperative and a condominium.

27. How can a partnership be dissolved?

28. Would a written promise to "pay $100 to bearer on the death of my Uncle Hodad" be negotiable? Explain.

29. What steps are necessary to negotiate an instrument made out to "bearer"?

30. What kind of trust can be affected by the doctrine of cy pres?

31. A contract that is so one-sided as to be unconscionable is called a(n)

      _____ .

32. The only way that a merchant can avoid making certain warranties is through a(n) _____ .

33. What is the name of the estate whose perpetual endurance depends upon each owner having children?

34. All of the following are rights of a surety except

    _____ indemnification
    _____ subrogation
    _____ exoneration
    _____ certification

35. Which of the following estates is the most extensive?

    _____ leasehold
    _____ fee tail
    _____ life estate
    _____ fee simple

36. Which of the following is a future interest in the grantor?

    _____ reversion
    _____ lease
    _____ remainder
    _____ habendum

37. Prescription works to the advantage of

    _____ the rightful owner.
    _____ the tenant.
    _____ the adverse possessor.
    _____ the druggist.

38. Rights on land owned by another are called

    _____ easements.
    _____ eminent domain.
    _____ prescription.
    _____ grants.

39. What capacity is required in order to be an agent?

    _____ contractual capacity
    _____ testamentary capacity
    _____ 5-quart capacity
    _____ no capacity

40. A check is not

_____ a negotiable instrument.
_____ commercial paper.
_____ a draft.
_____ a promissory note.

41. Perfection of a security interest may be accomplished by

_____ attachment of the interest.
_____ filing.
_____ transaction.
_____ practice.

42. Must a person have intent to kill to be guilty of murder?

43. How is burglary distinguished from criminal trespass?

44. A duly executed supplement to an existing will is called a(n)

_____ .

45. What term is used to describe promises or agreements entered into before a marriage?

46. What is the wrongful taking of property belonging to another called?
_____ What is it called if force is used?

_____

47. Which of the following is (are) necessary for a will to be valid?

_____ subscription.
_____ It must be all in the testator's handwriting.
_____ It must be nuncupative.
_____ The testator must have contractual capacity at the time he executes the will.

48. The trustor is the same as the

_____ cestui que trust.
_____ beneficiary.
_____ settlor.
_____ trustee.

49. Which of the following are homicides?

_____ murder
_____ voluntary manslaughter
_____ involuntary manslaughter
_____ felony murder

50. Which of the following crimes necessarily involve the intent to defraud?

_____ larceny
_____ forgery
_____ burglary
_____ robbery

ANSWERS

1. Subject matter jurisdiction and in rem jurisdiction. The court must always have subject matter jurisdiction before it can act. In a case like this, in rem jurisdiction is also needed. (Chapter 1, frame 2)

2. Invokes the court's jurisdiction and notifies the defendant. (Chapter 1, frame 3)

3. Venue. The others are all relevant to federal jurisdiction; the question of venue only arises once it has been determined that the court does, in fact, have jurisdiction. (Chapter 1, frame 4)

4. Answer and supplemental pleading. A reply is the plaintiff's response to the answer. Either party may file a supplemental pleading. (Chapter 1, frame 7)

5. It extends the jurisdiction of a state to people outside its borders. (Chapter 1, frame 2)

6. Personal service is preferred. Other methods are substituted and constructive service. (Chapter 1, frame 3)

7. Garnishment (Chapter 1, frame 3)

8. Relevance, materiality, and competence. They are the three basic requirements of admissible evidence. Some circumstantial evidence is admissible, some is not. (Chapter 2, frame 1)

9. None. They are all proper. (Chapter 2, frame 4)

10. A dying declaration. The hostility of a witness is relevant in determining what kinds of questions a lawyer may ask. (Chapter 2, frame 6)

11. Negligence, which, by its nature, is unintentional. (Chapter 3, frame 2)

12. Never. A counterclaim may be brought against the plaintiff by the defendant in a case. (Chapter 1, frame 6)

13. Res judicata prevents further litigation between the parties on a cause of action that has already been litigated; collateral estoppel prevents any future litigation by anyone on a particular point, once that point has been decided by a court. (Chapter 1, frame 9)

14. Venue. (Chapter 1, frame 5)

15. Cross-claim. (Chapter 1, frame 6)

16. Prima facie case. (Chapter 1, frame 7)

17. Judicial notice. (Chapter 2, frame 2)

18. Slander is spoken defamation; libel is written defamation. (Chapter 3, frame 7)

19. Actual. Punitive and exemplary damages are the same thing; there is no such thing (in this context, at least) as intentional damages. (Chapter 3, frame 1)

20. Contributory negligence, assumption of risk, and last clear chance. The doctrine of res ipsa loquitur works to the benefit of the plaintiff. (Chapter 3, frame 1)

21. Contracts. It is the rule that states that extrinsic evidence cannot be used to modify a written agreement. (Chapter 4, frame 1)

22. Fraud, minority of one party, and illegality. Unconscionability, not unprofitability, would invalidate the contract. (Chapter 4, frame 2)

23. Yes. When a merchant is involved, there is an implied warranty of merchantability. (Chapter 4, frame 4)

24. The rightful owner has the strongest claim. After that comes the finder, or, if it is found on privately owned land, the owner of the land. (Chapter 5, frame 1)

25. It can be any life (it need not be the holder of the estate). (Chapter 5, frame 2)

26. In a cooperative, the building is owned by a corporation, which is in turn owned by the occupants; each occupant of a condominium owns his own apartment, while all are joint owners of the common areas. (Chapter 5, frame 5)

27. Any change in the relationship (e.g., the withdrawal of one partner) can dissolve the partnership; any partner can, in fact, dissolve it at will. (Chapter 6, frame 2)

28. No. To be negotiable, a promissory note must specify time as well as an amount of money. Even if Uncle Hodad is not at all well, this promise is completely indefinite as to time. (Chapter 6, frame 5)

29. Only delivery. Indorsement would be needed if the instrument were payable to someone's order. (Chapter 6, frame 5)

30. Only a charitable trust. The doctrine is used to modify a trust that can no longer be carried out exactly. Modification is only made when it will be consistent with the apparent intent of the settlor. (Chapter 7, frame 5)

31. Adhesion contract. (Chapter 4, frame 2)

32. Disclaimer. (Chapter 4, frame 4)

33. Fee tail. (Chapter 5, frame 2)

34. Certification. A bank certifies checks. (Chapter 4, frame 5)

35. Fee simple. It has the potential to endure forever. (Chapter 5, frame 2)

36. Reversion. It is retained by the grantor when he transfers the property. (Chapter 5, frame 3)

37. The adverse possessor. Prescription is adverse possession. (The last choice may also be correct!) (Chapter 5, frame 4)

38. Easements. (They may be obtained by grant or prescription.) (Chapter 5, frame 6)

39. No capacity. Contractual capacity is required to appoint an agent. (Chapter 6, frame 1)

40. A promissory note. It is all of the others. (Chapter 6, frame 5)

41. Filing. It can also be accomplished by taking possession of the property in question. (Chapter 6, frame 7)

42. No. In fact, he needn't even be the actual killer. The felony murder rule makes each participant in a felony guilty of murder if during the crime one of them causes the death of a nonparticipant. (Chapter 8, frame 3)

43. Criminal trespass is the unlawful entering or remaining on property. For it to be burglary, the property must be a building and the actor must intend to commit a crime therein. (Chapter 8, frame 6)

44. Codicil. (Chapter 7, frame 3)

45. Antenuptial. (Chapter 7, frame 6)

46. Larceny; robbery. (Chapter 8, frame 7)

47. Subscription. The second choice applies to a holograph. The standard of testamentary capacity is actually lower than that of contractual capacity. (Chapter 7, frame 2)

48. Settlor. He is the person who creates the trust. (Chapter 7, frame 4)

49. They all are. A homicide is any culpable killing of another person. (Chapter 8, frame 3)

50. Forgery. The others may be committed without intent to defraud. (There may, of course, be other illicit intent.) (Chapter 8, frame 7)

Glossary of Legal Terms

Now, do you feel ready to translate from Legalese into English? Try this:

> When an ordinary man wants to give an orange to another, he would merely say, "I give you this orange." But when a lawyer does it, he says it this way: "Know all men by these presents that I hereby give, grant, bargain, sell, release, convey, transfer, and quitclaim all my right, title, interest, benefit, and use whatever in, of, and concerning this chattel, otherwise known as an orange, or citrus orantium, together with all the appurtenances thereto of skin, pulp, pip, rind, seeds, and juice for his own use and behoof, to himself and his heirs in fee simple forever, free from all liens, encumbrances, easements, limitations, restraints, or conditions whatsoever, now or anywhere made to the contrary notwithstanding, with full power to bite, cut, suck, or otherwise eat the said orange or to give away the same, with or without its skin, pulp, pip, rind, seeds, or juice."*

In case you feel as though you need some help, the following glossary contains many words not discussed in the preceding chapters. It will serve as a permanent reference on the subject of legal terminology. When you look up a word, though, remember that many are included in the chapters. If you wish to see if a particular word was discussed, check the index on page 157.

The abbreviations "n," "v," and "adj" are used to indicate "noun," "verb," and "adjective" in some cases where several definitions are given for one word. Words that come from languages other than English are so designated in parentheses.

---

*Originally appeared on page 51 of the *Community College Frontiers*, Vol. 5, No. 2, Winter, 1977. Contributed to the magazine by Lou Ridgeway, San Diego, CA. Reprinted with permission of *Community College Frontiers*.

A.B.A.   American Bar Association.

A.C.L.U.   American Civil Liberties Union.

A.L.I.   American Law Institute.

A fortiori *(Latin)*   Even more so; with stronger reason. If a particular item is true, then a fortiori, an included or lesser item is also true.

A posteriori *(Latin)*   From what comes after. Reasoning from experimental evidence and observation of the effect to determine the cause.

A priori *(Latin)*   From what goes before. Starting with general considerations and determining their effects.

Ab initio *(Latin)*   From the beginning; from the first act.

Abandon   To relinquish completely.

Abandonment   1. The complete relinquishment of property or rights without reference to any purpose or person.
2. Failure to proceed in a law suit for an extended period of time.
3. Desertion of children.
4. Unjustified separation of one spouse from the other.

Abatement   1. Reduction or decrease.
2. The suppression or removal of a nuisance.
3. Proportional reduction of legacies when there are insufficient funds to pay them totally.

Abduction   The illegal taking away by violence, fraud, or even persuasion of a child or wife. The consent of the person taken is not relevant. *See also* Kidnapping.

Abet   To give aid, particularly in commission of a crime.

Abettor   One who aids another in any way to commit a crime.

Abode   A dwelling place. *Compare with* Domicil(e).

Abrogate   To repeal or annul, e.g., to repeal a former rule or law.

Absolute   Unconditional; totally unrestricted.

Abstention   Practice of Federal Courts in refusing to decide cases, despite the fact that they have jurisdiction, where another remedy, specifically state law, is available.

Abstract   A summary. *Compare with* Transcript.

Abuse   1. (v) To injure by improper use.
2. (n) Improper use, e.g., of discretion or process.

Abut   To border upon or touch.

Acceptance   1. Agreement to an offer; the basis for a contract.
2. Signed promise of drawee of bill of exchange to honor the bill as it has been presented.
3. The certification of a check.

Accessory   A person connected with the commission of a crime but not present at the actual commission.

Accommodation   A favor. An accommodation indorser signs a bill or note in order to lend his name to another. (This would be called accommodation paper.)

Accomplice   One who voluntarily and knowingly aids in the commission of a crime.

Accord   An agreement. In contracts, agreement to settle a claim.

Accord and satisfaction   A fully executed accord.

Acquit   To discharge from an accusation, usually criminal.

Acquittal   Discharge from an accusation; a not-guilty verdict.

Action   A judicial proceeding.

Actionable   Providing the basis for a judicial proceeding.

Actual   Real; existing; not merely possible.

Actus *(Latin)*   An act (in civil law).

Actus reus *(Latin)*   Forbidden act.

Ad *(Latin)*   For; to; until; about; by.

Ad damnum *(Latin)*   To the damages; the clause in a complaint that describes and evaluates the plaintiff's damages.

Ad hoc *(Latin)*   For this; relevant to this case; for this particular purpose.

Ad hominum *(Latin)*   To the person, argument against the person instead of his reasoning.

Ad interim *(Latin)*   In the meantime.

Ad litem *(Latin)*   For the suit; during the suit; e.g., guardian ad litem.

Adeem   To take away, recall, or revoke.

Ademption   The satisfaction of a legacy, after the writing of a will, by some act of the testator. For example, the testator might, while still alive, give the amount of the legacy to the legatee. This would adeem (or satisfy) the gift in the will.

Adhesion contract   A one-sided contract presented by the stronger party and not bargained for by the weaker party.

Adjective law   Procedural law (as opposed to substantive law).

Adjourn   To postpone until a future session.

Adjudge   To decide or render judgment.

Adjudicate   To render judgment.

Administrative law   The branch of law dealing with the operation of the various governmental agencies that administer specific branches of the law.

Administrator The person who is appointed by the court to be the personal representative of the estate of a dead person.

Admissible Allowable in evidence.

Admission Voluntary statement by a party to a law suit supporting a position taken by the other side.

Adultery Sexual intercourse between a married person and another who is not his or her spouse.

Adversary proceeding A contested proceeding in which each side has an opportunity to be heard.

Adverse possession A method of gaining full legal title to land. The adverse possessor must hold the land openly and notoriously for a prescribed length of time. After holding the land for the statutory period, e.g., 10 years, the adverse possessor becomes the rightful owner.

Advisory opinion An opinion by a court on a question not officially before it for decision, e.g., submitted by a governmental body and not in a case at law.

Affiant A person who makes an affidavit.

Affidavit A written statement sworn to before a person who is legally permitted to administer an oath, e.g., a notary public.

Affirm To state solemnly; to ratify or confirm.

Affirmative defense A defense other than a denial of plaintiff's claims; a defense that brings in new material and that could be successful even if everything plaintiff claims is true.

Aforesaid Mentioned earlier.

Aforethought Premeditation.

After-acquired Acquired later than a certain time.

After-born Born after the death of the father.

Agency A fiduciary relationship in which one person is given the authority to represent another.

Agent A person authorized by another to represent him.

Aid and abet Advise, help, or encourage another to commit a crime.

Allegation An assertion; what one intends to prove.

Allege To state; to charge.

Alternative pleading A pleading that asserts contradictory theories so that if one fails, the other is tested, e.g., I did not hit you but, assuming that I did hit you, I was justified in doing so.

Ambit Border or boundary.

Amend To modify and improve.

Amendment   A correction or revision.

Amicus curiae *(Latin)*   Friend of the court; a person who advises the court although he is not a party to the action at hand.

Amnesty   A general forgiving for past offenses, usually granted for a class rather than an individual.

Ancillary   Auxiliary; supplementary.

Annuity   Periodic payments of a certain sum of money for either a fixed period of time or for the life of the recipient.

Annulment   The act of voiding something; e.g., when a marriage is annulled, it is as if it had never happened. (A divorce, on the other hand, terminates a marriage, but the record of the marriage remains.)

Answer   In pleading, the defendant's response to the complaint. The answer may deny part or all of the complaint, or it may bring up any affirmative defenses the defendant may have.

Antenuptial   Prior to marriage.

Apparent authority   Authority not actually granted by principal to agent, but represented by the principal to some third party in such a way that the third party believes that the agent has authority to act for the principal.

Appeal   To seek in a higher court review of a lower court decision.

Appear   To be before a court; to submit to the jurisdiction of a court.

Appellant   One who appeals a judgment.

Appellate   Having to do with an appeal. An appellate court is one that hears appeals.

Appellee   The party against whom a judgment is appealed.

Apportion   To distribute shares proportionally.

Arbiter   A private person granted by the parties to a dispute the power to settle the dispute.

Arbitrary   Capricious; according to whim rather than logic or reason.

Arbitration   A means of settling a dispute without judicial process, in which both sides are presented to an impartial third party, who may conduct an investigation and a hearing and then render a decision.

Arbitrator   A person who acts as the impartial third party in an arbitration. *See also* Arbiter.

Arguendo *(Latin)*   For the sake of argument.

Arm's length   An arm's length bargain is bargained for equally by both sides; neither side has an unfair advantage over the other.

Arraign   To prepare a defendant for trial by bringing him into court to hear the charges and to enter his plea.

Arrest   The taking into custody of a person, depriving him of some freedom under legal authority or color of legal authority.

Arson   The deliberate burning of a building.

As per   In accordance with.

Assault   The placing of another in immediate fear of physical harm as a result of threatening gestures. The key element is that the victim must actually apprehend the harm. In many jurisdictions, criminal assault actually requires some physical injury.

Assent   1. (n) Agreement.
            2. (v) To agree.

Assess   To fix the value of some property, usually for purposes of taxation. To call for contributions from the various members of a group.

Assets   Property of any kind whatsoever, e.g., money, stock, personal property.

Assign   To transfer to another, e.g., to assign property to some interest therein.

Assignee   A person to whom an assignment is made.

Assignment   A transfer to another of property or rights.

Assignor   A person who makes an assignment.

Assigns   Assignees.

Assise   *See* Assize.

Assize   An old English court. Also, the verdict of that court, a writ, an action, and many other meanings.

Assumption   Taking over or taking upon oneself, e.g., assumption of a debt.

Assumption of risk   Exposing oneself to danger of which one has prior knowledge. This may negate the liability of the one who has created the danger.

Assure   To ensure; to make certain; to put beyond doubt.

Attach   To bring property under custody of a court.

Attachment   1. The act of seizing property, through legal channels, in order to bring it under the custody of the court.
               2. The creation of a security interest.

Attainder   At ancient common law, deprivation of rights of a person sentenced to death, including forfeiture of all property. A bill of attainder, which is unconstitutional in the United States, was an act of the legislature that declared a person guilty of a capital crime (without a trial).

Attempt   An inchoate crime; must include an overt act done with the intent to commit the crime. It is more than mere contemplation or planning.

Attest To affirm; to certify; to bear witness to.

Attestation clause The clause of a will in which witnesses certify that the will was properly executed.

Attractive nuisance A condition on property which is likely to attract small children but which is also dangerous to them. One who possesses property containing such a condition must take precautions to prevent injury to children.

Authority 1. Legal precedent.

2. The power of an agent to act for his principal.

Autre *(French)* Another.

Autre vie *(French)* Another life.

Award 1. The decision of an arbitrator.

2. A judgment for payment of costs or damages.

Bad faith The opposite of good faith; involving deliberate and intentional action with some ulterior motive, be it ill will or self-interest.

Bail Money paid to secure the release of a prisoner from jail. Should the prisoner then fail to appear at trial, the money is forfeited.

Bailee A person to whom a bailment is made.

Bailiff A court official whose function is to help maintain order.

Bailment Entrustment of property by the owner to another person, usually for a specific purpose, e.g., storing an automobile in a garage.

Bailor A person who makes a bailment.

Bankruptcy The law under which an insolvent debtor may be discharged from his debts by bringing all his assets into court.

Bar 1. The railing that encloses the officers of the court.

2. All attorneys who are admitted to practice before a court.

Battery The intentional unlawful touching of one person by another person or by an object controlled or set in motion by the other person.

Bearer A person who holds a negotiable instrument that is payable to whoever holds it, usually payable to "cash" or to "bearer."

Bench 1. The seat upon which judges sit.

2. The judges of a court collectively.

Beneficiary A person who receives a benefit as a result of a gift, a trust, a will, etc.

Bequeath To give personal property by will. *See also* Devise.

Bequest A gift by will of personal property, a legacy.

Bias Prejudice; preconception that makes it difficult or impossible to be fair.

Bigamy   The crime of someone marrying a second time while already a party to a valid marriage.

Bilateral contract   Contract in which both parties agree to do something (as opposed to unilateral contract).

Bill   1. A formal complaint in a lawsuit.
2. A law, as passed by a legislative body.
3. A negotiable instrument, e.g., a bank note.

Bill of exchange   A written order from one person to another to pay money to a third person.

Bill of particulars   A written specification by the plaintiff of matters that have been set forth in the original pleading.

Bill of rights   The first ten amendments of the U.S. Constitution.

Black letter law   Principles of law that are so basic as to be almost universally accepted.

Blackmail   The crime of extortion of money by threat, usually threat of exposure of some conduct of the victim.

Blue law   A strict law regulating conduct of the Sabbath.

Blue ribbon jury   A jury of specially qualified jurors.

Blue sky law   Law regulating the sale of securities with the intent of preventing fraud.

Board of directors   The governing body of a private corporation.

Bona fide *(Latin)*   Acting in or with good faith.

Breach   A breaking or a violation of a law, contract, duty, or warranty.

Brief   A written statement of position prepared by each side in a lawsuit.

Burden of proof   The duty of proving to the court that one's assertions are in fact the truth by showing that the evidence favors them.

Burglary   At common law, the illegal entry, at night, of a dwelling with the intent to commit a felony once inside. Modern laws tend to eliminate one or more of the common law requirements.

Buyer   The party to whom property is transferred in a contract of sale.

By-laws   Rules for running a corporation or other business or society.

C.A.   Court of appeals.

C.C.   Circuit court.

C.J.   1. Chief justice or chief judge.
2. Circuit judge.

C.P.A.   Certified public accountant.

Calendar   In a court, the list of cases for trial.

Cancellation   Termination of a contract by agreement of the parties or because one side has breached the contract.

Canon   A rule or law.

Capacity   Legal competency, e.g., to act, to sue, to understand.

Capital   Assets used to make money. Total capital is the net worth of a corporation; stated capital is the total par value of the shares sold.

Capital crime   Crime that may be punished by death.

Carrier   A transporter of persons or property.

Cartel   A group of companies, usually in the same general business, associated together for some improper purpose, such as price fixing.

Case   A lawsuit. *See also* Trespass on the case.

Case law   The aggregate of reported cases (as opposed to statute law).

Cashier   An employee who is in charge of operating a cash register. In a bank, the cashier is an executive officer, often the chief executive officer, who is responsible for the bank's cash.

Causa mortis *(Latin)*   In contemplation of death. A gift causa mortis is a gift given in contemplation of death and takes effect only upon the death of the donor.

Cause of action   The right to start a lawsuit or the facts that give rise to such a right.

Caveat *(Latin)*   A warning to beware.

Caveat actor *(Latin)*   Let the actor or doer beware.

Caveat emptor *(Latin)*   Let the buyer beware.

Certificate   Formal written authentication of some fact or circumstance.

Certified check   A check that the bank accepts in advance, thereby guaranteeing that it is good.

Certiorari *(Latin)*   Voluntary review of a decision by a higher court; distinguished from an appeal, which is heard as a matter of right.

Cestui que trust *(Anglo–French)*   The person who is the beneficiary of the trust.

Chain of title   All successive changes in the ownership of a piece of real property.

Chambers   The private office of a judge, near but not actually part of the court, where some of the court's business is conducted.

Chancellor   Originally, the highest judicial officer in England. A judge of a chancery court.

Chancery   A court of equity jurisprudence. Today, American courts of law and equity have merged.

Charge 1. (v) To accuse.

2. (n) The judge's instructions to the jury on matters of law.

Chattel mortgage A mortgage on personal property.

Chattels Personal property; movable property (not land).

Check An order to a bank for payment of money to a named payee or bearer. A type of negotiable instrument.

Chose *(French)* Literally, a thing; a cause of action.

Chose in action A right to be paid, recoverable by bringing an action.

Circuit court Court whose jurisdiction is wider than just one district. The name is derived from the fact that early judges "rode circuit" in order to serve their entire jurisdiction.

Circumstantial evidence Indirect evidence; involves the use of the existence of one fact because it implies the truth of the conclusion desired to be proved.

Citation 1. A summons or a writ commanding a person to appear in court.

2. A reference to existing legal authority in order to strengthen an argument or a position advanced.

Civil Pertaining to the community.

Civil action A noncriminal court action, a lawsuit contested between two citizens to enforce a right or obtain redress for some wrong.

Civil death Common law extinction of all civil rights that takes place upon conviction of a felony. It no longer exists in most states.

Civil law Roman law and its derivatives; law based on a code.

Civil rights The legal rights of individuals as guaranteed by the Constitution.

Class action An action brought by a small number of named plaintiffs on behalf of a larger group, all with similar causes of action.

Clean hands An equitable doctrine that prevents a person from seeking equitable relief unless he has acted properly with regard to the matter being adjudicated.

Clear and present danger The test of whether spoken words may be without the protection of the Constitution. Such words are unprotected only if they do create a clear and present danger of serious violence.

Clerk A person who keeps records for another. A clerk of the court is responsible for keeping the court's records.

Close corporation Corporation ownership that is limited to a few shareholders.

Closed shop A job location where only members of a specific union may work.

Code   A published set of laws, usually arranged according to some numerical system of subdivisions.

Code civil   The codification of French civil law; undertaken under Napoleon I; also called Code Napoleon or Napoleonic Code.

Codicil   A supplement, change, or addition to a will.

Coercion   Compulsion of a person to do something against his or her will; may be accomplished by force or persuasion.

Collateral   At or from the side; money or other property offered as security for a loan.

Collateral attack   Indirect attack; an attack on a judgment by way of a proceeding which has a primary purpose other than attacking the judgment.

Collateral estoppel   The doctrine that bars a court from making a determination as to facts that have already been determined by a competent court.

Collective bargaining   The required bargaining between an employer and a union representing the employees.

Color   Semblance; appearance; e.g., color of law (not necessarily under actual authority of law).

Comity   Courtesy; recognition by one state or nation of the laws of another.

Commerce   All forms of trade and commercial intercourse.

Commerce clause   Article I, Section 8, of the U.S. Constitution; it allows Congress to control all interstate and international trade.

Commercial paper   Negotiable instruments.

Committee   1. A group selected to perform a particular duty.
2. The guardian of an incompetent person.

Common law   Judge or court-made law that receives its binding force from custom, usage, and judicial decisions (as distinguished from legislation). It originated in early England and is constantly evolving.

Common law marriage   A marriage that takes place without ceremony but solely because the parties live together as husband and wife for a certain amount of time.

Community property   Property owned jointly by a husband and wife; in some states, all property acquired during the marriage is community property.

Comparative negligence   Rule under which the negligence of plaintiff is compared to that of defendant to determine how much plaintiff is entitled to recover. *Compare with* Contributory negligence.

Competent   Adequate, qualified.

Competent court   Having lawful jurisdiction.

Competent evidence   Relevant, proper, and admissible.

Competent witness   A witness who meets certain standards, such as age, intelligence, and ability to comprehend the importance of telling the truth.

Complaint   In civil practice, a pleading setting out the cause of action; in criminal law, the formal charge.

Concur   To agree, to act together.

Concurrent   At the same time, e.g., two courts have concurrent jurisdiction when they each have jurisdiction to hear the same matter; two sentences of imprisonment are concurrent if they can be served at the same time instead of consecutively.

Condemnation   1. Exercise of the power of eminent domain; the taking of private property (with compensation to the owner) for public use.
2. The declaration that a building is unfit for use.
3. A finding of guilt.

Condition   A provision in a contract that modifies rights or duties under the contract if a certain event takes place.

Condominium   Joint ownership of a multiple dwelling in such a way that each dweller has sole ownership of an individual apartment and all are joint owners of the common areas.

Confession   An admission of guilt of a crime.

Confidentiality   Requirement that the privacy of certain relationships (lawyer–client, doctor–patient, etc.) receive legal protection. For example, a lawyer may not repeat information obtained in confidence from a client.

Conflict of laws   The area of the law that governs when one nation or state will apply the laws of another.

Conjugal   Having to do with marriage.

Consanguinity   Blood relationship, kinship.

Consent   1. (n) Voluntary agreement.
2. (v) To agree voluntarily.

Consideration   Inducement to a contract; the thing that is bargained for in a contract; that which is given by one party in exchange for the promise of the other party. Without consideration, there can be no valid contract.

Consignment   The turning over of goods to another for transportation or for sale. Title is retained by the consignor.

Consolidation   The trying of two or more different related cases as one case.

Conspiracy A criminal offense consisting of the joining of two or more persons for the purpose of doing an unlawful act.

Constitution General and basic set of laws and principles of government of a nation or state that may be either written or unwritten. The U.S. Constitution, adopted in 1787, is the supreme law of the land.

Constitutional In agreement with or consistent with the Constitution.

Constitutional law The study of the application and interpretation of the Constitution.

Constitutional right A right guaranteed by the Constitution; cannot be tampered with by more legislation.

Construction Determination of the meaning of words in a constitution, law, contract, etc., by considering the meanings of the words themselves and also all of the surrounding circumstances. It is more than just interpretation, which employs only consideration of the words themselves.

Constructive Considered to be the case even though not actually so.

Constructive eviction Eviction in effect; while the landlord has not actually evicted the tenant, the condition of the property has reached a state where it is no longer livable, so that the tenant might as well have been evicted.

Constructive notice Not actual notice. Where actual notice is not possible, such notice as the law deems sufficient, e.g., published in a newspaper.

Constructive trust A trust established by law when the legal owner of property gained title improperly, and in the interests of fairness the legal owner is deemed to hold the property in trust for another.

Construe To interpret.

Contemporaneous At the same time.

Contempt A manifestation of disrespect for a court or a legislature, including a deliberate refusal to obey an order of such a court or legislature.

Contingent Possible but not absolutely certain to happen; depending on some other event, e.g., an attorney's contingent fee depends on the outcome of the case.

Continuance An adjournment, i.e., of an action pending in court.

Contra *(Latin)* Contrary to; against; in opposition to.

Contraband Anything it is against the law to own or to transport, e.g., narcotics.

Contract An agreement, supported by consideration and not contrary to any law, to do or not to do some act. A contract may be written or oral.

Contractor A person who enters a contract.

Contributory negligence   Rule under which any negligence on the part of the plaintiff precludes recovering any damage from the defendant, even though the defendant was also negligent. *Compare with* Comparative negligence.

Conversion   1. A wrongful act of ownership exercised over the property of another.
2. Changing one type of property to another; equitable conversion is the exchange of real property for personal property.

Conveyance   A deed transferring title to real property.

Convict   To find guilty.

Conviction   An adjudication of guilt by a verdict or by a guilty plea.

Cooling time *(Cooling-off period)*   Time to calm down after provocation; a waiting period prescribed by law before commencing a strike or a divorce action.

Cooperative   A multiple dwelling owned by a corporation, which is in turn owned by the residents of the building.

Copyright   The right of the author, artist, etc., to control publication of his work. Copyrights are regulated by federal law.

Corespondent   The third party in a divorce action based on adultery.

Corporal punishment   Physical punishment.

Corporation   An artificial entity created by law strictly for business purposes and owned through purchase of corporate stock. It is liable only to the extent of the corporate assets, not the personal wealth of the owners.

Corpus *(Latin)*   Literally, the body. An aggregate or mass, e.g., of men, laws, or articles.

Corpus delicti *(Latin)*   Body of the crime; the actual item that was the subject of the crime; e.g., in a murder, the corpus delicti is the corpse.

Corpus juris *(Latin)*   The body of the law.

Corroborate   To support; to add credibility. Corroborating evidence supports that which has already been heard.

Costs   The expenses of the successful party in a court action ordered to be paid by the losing party.

Council   A municipal legislature.

Counsel, counsellor   A lawyer.

Count   Each item of a complaint or indictment; each states a separate cause of action.

Counterclaim   A claim by the defendant against the plaintiff in a civil suit.

Course   The ordinary or usual way in which something moves.

Course of business The ordinary or usual running of the business.

Court 1. The governmental organ that dispenses justice.
       2. The judge himself.
       3. The place where the judge exercises his judicial function.

Court of appeals A court that hears appeals after a trial has been completed in a lower court. In most jurisdictions it is a middle-level court, but in some states, such as New York, it is the highest court.

Court of chancery An equity court, a court with the same jurisdiction as a chancellor. In America today, the courts have jurisdiction in both law and equity.

Court of claims A federal court that hears all claims against the United States.

Court of law A court administering the laws and statutes. In America today, the courts of law and equity have merged.

Court of probate A court with jurisdiction to probate wills, estates, etc.

Covenant Agreement contained in a deed which binds the buyer, the seller, or both. Some covenants are said to "run with the land" and bind all future purchasers (as opposed to only the party to the original covenant): e.g., covenant against encumbrances, which means that there are no outstanding interests against title to the land; or a covenant of quiet enjoyment, which assures buyer that seller will protect buyer from eviction by others claiming title.

Coverture Formerly, the status of a married woman, including certain special rights and restrictions (now archaic).

Credible Worthy of belief.

Credit Money due to be received.

Creditor A person who is owed money by another (the debtor).

Crime An offense against the state; a violation of the penal law.

Criminal 1. (adj) Having to do with crime.
         2. (n) A person who has committed a crime.

Criminal law Branch of the law dealing with crimes.

Criminal mischief Intentional or reckless damage to property.

Criminal trespass Unlawfully entering or remaining on property.

Cross-claim A claim by one co-defendant against another, related to the main suit.

Cross-examination The questioning of a witness for the opposition in order to test the truth of his statements.

Culpable Criminal; censurable; blamable.

Curtesy The common law right of a husband in the real property of his wife. (The wife's right in her husband's property is called dower.) Today, each spouse has the same rights to the property of the other.

Custody Control; care; keeping.

Custom A practice so well established that it takes on legal importance.

Cy pres *(French)* As near as possible. When a charitable gift cannot be carried out exactly, the court will alter it so as to carry it out as nearly as possible. This is the doctrine of cy pres.

D.A. District attorney.

D.B.A. Doing business as, usually written d/b/a.

D.C. District of Columbia.

D.J. District judge.

Damages Money awarded by a court as compensation for an injury or wrong caused by another. They are classed as (1) actual or compensatory —as compensation for the actual injury, or (2) punitive (exemplary)—in excess of the actual damage, but intended as punishment.

Damnum *(Latin)* Damages or loss.

Dangerous instrumentality Something that is inherently dangerous, sometimes allowing for liability without actual fault on the part of the owner.

Dangerous weapon A weapon capable of killing.

De *(Latin, French)* Of; from; concerning.

De facto *(Latin)* In fact (even if not by law); e.g., de facto segregation existed even where no legal plan to segregate any longer existed; a business may be a de facto corporation even though it has failed to meet one of the small requirements of the law.

De jure *(Latin)* By law; by right; valid in the eyes of the law.

De novo *(Latin)* New; over again.

Deadly weapon A weapon designed to cause death.

Death The moment when life ends, the state of being dead. When a person is inexplicably absent for a certain period, usually 7 years, that person is presumed dead.

Debenture A corporate bond, usually unsecured by any property.

Debit Money owing; to be paid out.

Debt Money that is owed according to some definite agreement.

Debtor A person who owes something to another person.

Decedent A person who has died; a deceased person.

Deceit An intentional falsehood causing harm to another; a type of fraud.

Decision The formal resolution by a judge of a lawsuit; the written report of that finding.

Declarant A person who makes a statement (declaration) that may later be evidence.

Declaration A statement in evidence made by someone who is not available as a witness. Some declarations are given more credence than others, e.g., a declaration against interest (a statement adverse to the interests of the declarant at the time the statement was made) and a dying declaration (statement made while in extremis, relevant to the wrongful cause of death, such as in a homicide) are both given extra credence.

Declaratory judgment A judgment that answers a legal question without ordering that any action be taken or damages be enforced; it simply defines the rights of the parties. There must, however, be some actual dispute at issue.

Decree A judgment in an equitable action.

Deductible Something that may be used as a deduction for income tax purposes.

Deduction Something that one is allowed to subtract from one's total income for tax purposes, e.g., charitable contributions. Deductions also exist in estate taxation.

Deed A signed document stating the transfer of a piece of real property.

Defamation Oral (slander) or written (libel) published statements injurious to the reputation of another. In order to be actionable, the statements must be false.

Defamatory Bringing about defamation.

Default An omission or failure to perform a legal duty; failure to make a required payment or to appear or take a necessary step in a lawsuit.

Default judgment A judgment entered against a defendant who is in default.

Defeasible Subject to being defeated or annulled if some future event takes place.

Defect An absence of some necessary part or legal requirement.

Defendant The person against whom the suit is brought.

Defense That which is brought forth by the defendant.

Defraud To commit acts of fraud, to cheat.

Delictum *(Latin)* A wrong.

Delivery Transfer of possession or control of an item from one person to another.

Demand   A claim for performance of a legal obligation.

Demand note   Promissory note payable on demand (or at once).

Demise   To convey, to lease.

Demur   To interpose a demurrer.

Demurrer   A common law pleading which, assuming for the sake of argument that everything in the complaint is true, says that there still exists no basis for a recovery. In other words, a demurrer questions the legal sufficiency of the complaint.

Denial   In pleading, a refutation of the claims made by the opponent; a refusal or a withholding.

Dependent   A person who is supported by another.

Deponent   A person who makes a deposition.

Deposition   A written statement, given under oath, usually outside of court for use in court.

Depreciation   A drop in value. A certain amount of depreciation can sometimes be used as a tax deduction.

Descendant   A person who proceeds from the body of any ancestor, no matter how remote.

Descent   An inheritance from any ancestors.

Desertion   The abandonment of a post of duty or of a spouse or child.

Determination   A ruling of a court.

Detriment   Harm or loss.

Devise   Gift by will of real estate.

Dicta   *See* Dictum.

Dictum *(Latin; plural: dicta)*   A digression in the court's opinion, not necessary to explain the holding in the case at hand.

Digest   A collection of numerous books or materials in one volume for facility of reference.

Dilatory   Delaying, causing delay.

Diligence   Care and prudence.

Direct   Immediate; not remote.

Direct evidence   Proof of the fact in question without reference to other facts.

Direct examination   The first questioning of a witness by the party who called that witness.

Directed verdict   Jury verdict ordered by the judge, thus making it unnecessary for the jury to reach its own verdict.

Disability   A state of weakness or incapacity; lack of legal capacity.

Disbar To revoke a lawyer's license to practice law.

Discharge To release; to terminate.

Discharge in bankruptcy To release a bankrupt from all debts, except those excluded for some reason.

Disclaimer A refusal to accept responsibility, a renunciation.

Discontinuance The cessation or termination of an action.

Discovery The process by which the adverse parties in a lawsuit exchange information necessary for the trying of the suit.

Disinterested Impartial; having no personal interest in the outcome.

Dismiss To order a lawsuit ended or a motion denied.

Dismissal An order ending a lawsuit without an actual trial, having the same effect as a judgment against the plaintiff. Sometimes a plaintiff may seek a voluntary dismissal without prejudice, meaning the suit can be brought again at a later date. If the dismissal is with prejudice, such a later suit is precluded.

Dissent 1. (v) To disagree.
2. (n) The formal minority opinion of a judge who does not agree with the majority.

Dissolution The breaking up, dissolving, splitting up into original component parts, or canceling of something, e.g., a corporation.

Distrain To take the property of another and hold it until he performs some obligation.

Distress The act or process of distraining.

Diversity of citizenship One basis for federal jurisdiction, where the controversy is between citizens of different states.

Dividend A gain, a share of some property, a payment by a corporation to shareholders.

Divorce The ending of a marriage by order of the court. *Compare with* Annulment.

Docket A list or record of cases of a particular court.

Document Anything that records information.

Documentary evidence Tangible evidence in the form of a document.

Doing business A term that signifies that an out-of-state corporation has performed enough acts within the state to fall under the jurisdiction of the state for purposes of being sued and taxed.

Domicil(e) *(Latin)* The place where a person makes his permanent home, to which he plans eventually to return. While a person may have several residences, he can have only one domicile at a given time.

Donee The recipient of a gift.

Donor The giver of a gift.

Double jeopardy The trying of a person twice for the same offense. This is prohibited by the fifth amendment to the Constitution.

Doubt Uncertainty. In order to render a verdict of guilty in a criminal case, the jury must be certain "beyond a reasonable doubt."

Dower The common law right of a wife in the real property of her husband. *See also* Curtesy.

Draft A negotiable instrument that contains a written order from one person (the drawer) to another (the drawee) to pay money to a third person (the payee); a bill of exchange.

Drawee The party to whom a bill of exchange is advanced.

Drawer The party who writes a bill of exchange.

Duces tecum *(Latin)* Literally, bring with you. *See also* Subpoena duces tecum.

Due care Sufficient care under the circumstances.

Due process of law One of the most difficult concepts to define; the main idea is fairness. It always includes fair notice and a chance to be heard.

Duress The wrongful compulsion of a person to do an act he would not otherwise have done. It may take the form of violence, restraint, threats, etc.

Duty An obligation, legal or contractual; a tax on items imported into a country.

Dwelling house A residence or abode.

Dying declaration A statement by the victim of a homicide relating to the homicide, made while the victim is dying.

E.B.T. Examination before trial; questioning of party to lawsuit by opposition as part of discovery procedure.

E.G. *See* Exempli gratia.

Earned income Income obtained as a result of work or other efforts of the person to whom it is paid, rather than money merely paid to a person, such as dividends on stock. Simply, money earned from labor, not capital.

Easement The right of one person to use the land of another for a specified purpose. An example would be a right-of-way across a neighbor's land in order to reach a road.

Ecclesiastical Pertaining to religion or the church.

Effects Personal property.

Ejectment A common law action to recover land.

Election The act of choosing, be it in (1) political voting, (2) filing a tax return, or (3) choosing between inheriting under a will or taking a minimum prescribed legal inheritance.

Elector A member of the electoral college; a voter.

Electoral College The presidential electors; the people selected by the voters of each state to elect the president and vice-president of the United States.

Emancipation The setting free or liberation of some person or persons from parental control or some form of bondage.

Embezzlement The fraudulent taking of money that has been entrusted to the taker, who may be a trustee or an employee in a position to alter financial records.

Emigration The leaving of one's country in order to move to another.

Eminent domain The power of the government to take private property for public use by compensating the owner.

Employ To hire or engage the services of another person.

Employee A person who works for another (the employer) and who is under the control of the employer; a servant.

Employer A person who hires another and directs him in his work; a master.

Employment A job; the act of being employed or of employing.

Emptor *(Latin)* A buyer.

Enact To decree; to establish by law.

Encroach To trespass, to accomplish an encroachment.

Encroachment An intrusion onto the property of another, e.g., a fence that extends onto a neighbor's property.

Encumber To place land under an encumbrance.

Encumbrance Any impediment that lessens the value of land (such as a mortgage).

Endorse *See* Indorse.

Enjoin To order or command, to forbid or issue an injunction.

Entail To create an estate in tail, an estate that is limited in the way it can pass to future generations. *See* Fee tail.

Enter To make an entry or a record. Entering judgment is the formal recording of the court's decision.

Entirety The totality. The joint estate of a married couple is called estate by the entirety.

Entrapment   An inducement by police to entice a person to commit a crime that he would not otherwise have committed. A person who has been so lured can use that fact in his defense.

Entry   1. Unlawful entering of a building in order to commit a crime therein.

2. The act of making a record or the record itself.

Equal protection of the laws   A fourteenth amendment right which forbids denial to some people of protections that are accorded to others, the denial being based on race, color, creed, etc.

Equitable   1. Just; fair.

2. Emanating from a court of equity.

Equitable conversion   The exchange of real property for personal property by a court of equity.

Equity   A word with broad meanings, mostly centering around fairness and the court's power to do what is right in the situation; or to act even when no remedy exists at law. Courts of equity (also called courts of chancery) are now merged with courts of law; one court has both powers.

Error   A mistake by a court made in trying a case. It may be a mistake of law or of fact, and it may or may not be serious enough to upset the judgment on appeal. If so, it is called reversible error; if not, a harmless error.

Escalator clause   A contract clause, usually in a contract for sale or rental which allows the contract price to be raised if certain events take place, e.g., rising costs or raising of the legal maximum.

Escheat   The passing to the state of property that has no legal owner, e.g., on the death of a person with no heirs and no will.

Escrow   The holding of some property or papers by a disinterested third party, delivery of the escrow items being contingent on some performance by the person to whom the items are eventually to be delivered.

Esquire   A title formally applied to lawyers.

Estate   1. The interest of a person in a piece of real property measured by potential duration, e.g., for life; the property itself.

2. The total of all of a dead person's property (decedent's estate).

Estate at sufferance   The interest of a tenant who remains on property after his right to be there has expired.

Estate at will   A leasehold estate that can be terminated at the will of either party.

Estate for life   *See* Life estate.

Estate for years An estate that ends after a specific amount of time.

Estop To bar or prevent; to stop.

Estoppel A bar that prevents a person from asserting something, even though it may be true. An estoppel usually arises as a result of some prior act, assertion, or promise by the person being estopped.

Et *(Latin, French)* And.

Et al. *(Latin)* An abbreviation for et alius, meaning "and another," or for et alii, meaning "and others."

Et seq. *(Latin)* An abbreviation for et sequitur, meaning "and as follows"; "and the following pages."

Et ux. *(Latin)* An abbreviation for et uxor, meaning "and wife."

Euthanasia Mercy killing.

Eviction Dispossession, particularly of tenant by landlord.

Evidence Information presented in court through which the truth is to be determined. The rules of evidence determine which evidence is admissible and which is not.

Ex *(Latin)* From; out of; by; former.

Ex officio *(Latin)* By virtue of the power of the office.

Ex parte *(Latin)* By one side or party (without the presence of the other).

Ex post facto *(Latin)* After the act or fact. An ex post facto law, which is unconstitutional, makes an act a crime subject to punishment even though it was not considered criminal when it was committed.

Examination An inspection; questioning, especially under oath.

Exception 1. An exclusion.
2. A statement of objection to a judge's ruling during trial to be decided at a later time.

Exchange 1. (v) To trade or swap.
2. (n) A forum for trading or swapping.

Excise tax A tax on the sale or use of any item or on any activity.

Exclusionary rule The rule that prevents illegally obtained evidence from being admitted in a criminal case.

Exclusive Sole and undivided; not allowing any others.

Exculpatory Relieving of guilt or responsibility.

Execute 1. To complete; to make valid; to carry out.
2. To put to death by order of law.

Executor The person chosen by a person making a will to carry out the will by following the instructions therein for distribution of the estate.

Executory Still to be executed or performed to some extent.

Exempli gratia *(Latin)* For example. Abbreviated "e.g.".

Exempt Free of some obligation (such as military service).

Exemption 1. Freedom from some obligation.
2. A specific amount of money, prescribed by law, to be subtracted from income in computing tax. Each family member receives an exemption.

Exhibit Anything offered as evidence at a trial.

Exigency Urgency.

Exoneration A release from a burden or absolution from a charge of criminal conduct.

Expert witness A person who is so knowledgeable on a subject that he is allowed to testify as to his conclusions. An ordinary witness is allowed to testify only to facts.

Expiration An ending due to passage of time.

Express Explicit; clear. For example, express authority is established when one person tells another that he has authority to act on his behalf.

Expropriate To condemn, or to take private property for public use.

Expulsion The driving out of someone or something.

Expunge To obliterate; to erase; to wipe out.

Extension A lengthening, either physical (an extension to a house) or chronological (extension of a lease or a time to reply to a motion).

Extenuating circumstances Facts that tend to excuse misconduct and are taken into account in determining punishment.

Extinguishment Termination, e.g., of a right or a property interest.

Extort To compel by illegal threats.

Extortion Compulsion by force or threats, usually to pay some money.

Extra *(Latin)* Beyond, outside of.

Extradition The transfer of a person accused of a crime to the place where he is accused from some other state or nation.

Extrahazardous Extremely dangerous.

Extraordinary Unusual; rare.

Extremis *(Latin)* At the point of death; in the final illness from which there is virtually no chance of recovery.

Extrinsic From the outside; foreign; from other sources.

Eyewitness A person who is able to testify as to what he has actually seen or heard.

F.C.C. Federal Communications Commission.

F.O.B. *See* Free on board.

F.T.C.   Federal Trade Commission.

Fabricate   To create or falsify.

Face   Whatever appears in the actual language of a paper or document. *See also* Four corners.

Facsimile   An exact copy of something.

Fact   Something that is real and true, which exists or has happened.

Factor   A person who buys and sells goods for others on a commission basis. One who finances accounts receivable, usually for a percentage of the sales.

Factum *(Latin)*   Fact.

Fair   Equitable, reasonable, and proper.

Fair consideration   A reasonable equivalent, more than just nominal.

Fair hearing   A hearing held in accordance with certain fundamental rules of justice and fair play.   *Xét xử ı được công chức*

Fair market value   The actual value; the price that would be arrived at by an equally anxious buyer and seller.

Fair trial   A trial held in accordance with the law in an impartial atmosphere.

Fair value   The present actual value.

False   Untrue, particularly unintentionally.

False arrest   The unlawful restraint of one person by another.   *Bắt uẹ trái phạy!*

False entry   An entry in the financial accounts of a bank which is intentionally made incorrectly with the intention of defrauding the bank.

False imprisonment   Unlawful restraint of one person by another.   *giam giữ trái phạy,*

False pretenses   A misrepresentation used to defraud another.   *Dối gạt*

Falsehood   A willful lie designed to deceive another.   *Lừa dối*

Family   A word whose meaning varies depending on the context in which it is used; usually describing a group of persons who are related to each other or who live together as a unit.

Fault   A wrongful act, omission, or breach; a failure to do what is necessary; negligence.   *Lỗi , quá thất*

Fear   The apprehension or anxiety caused by actual or supposed danger.

Feasible   Possible; capable of happening.

Feasor   A doer; one who does.

Federal   Joined and having a common central government. In American law, federal government and laws are national as opposed to their state and local equivalents.

Federal question   A case or lawsuit that involves the U.S. Constitution or federal laws.

Fee   1. A charge for services.
  2. An estate (real property) without restrictions or alienation even after the death of the estate builder, when the estate passes to his heirs.

Fee simple   The most extensive estate in real property, capable of enduring forever. Also called fee simple absolute. *See also* Fee.

Fee tail   Same as fee simple except after death it can only be passed on to "heirs of the body" (children) of the owner.

Fellow servant   One who serves the same master or employer.

Fellow servant rule   A common law rule which at one time held the employer not liable for injuries caused by one employee to another.

Felon   A person who commits a felony.

Felonious   Done with intent to commit a felony; malicious; malignant.

Felony   A very serious crime, e.g., murder, robbery.

Felony murder rule   Any homicide committed during the commission of a felony is considered murder.

Feticide   The destruction of a fetus.

Fiction   A manufactured situation in which something possibly false is assumed to be true in order to advance the cause of justice.

Fictitious payee   A made-up (false) person to whom a negotiable instrument is made out with no intention that he shall ever actually be paid.

Fiduciary   1. A person who holds money or something of value in trust for another.
  2. A situation in which one person is trusted to act for another.

FIFO   *See* First in, first out.

File   1. (n) The record of a case.
  2. (v) To give any document to the appropriate public officer so that it becomes part of the permanent record of the office.

Filiation   The relation of parent and child.

Finding   A decision as to a question of fact. Also called finding of fact.

Fine   A sum of money paid as punishment by a person who has been found guilty of an offense.

First in, first out *(FIFO)*   A method of calculating the value of inventory wherein the items still in stock are always considered to be those most recently obtained.

Fiscal   Having to do with finances.

Fiscal year   A 12-month accounting period. The federal fiscal year runs from July 1 to June 30.

Fixture   An article that is physically attached to land and is therefore considered a part of it and cannot be removed.

Force   1. Physical power.
2. Wrongful violence.

Forced sale   A sale to pay off a judgment of court.

Forcible entry   1. Entry by breaking doors or windows.
2. Entry against the will of the owner.

Foreclosure   The total shutting out of the mortgagor by the mortgagee; it involves taking of the property and ending of all rights of the mortgagor. Foreclosure is generally a result of nonpayment of the mortgage.

Foreign   Of another state or nation.

Forensic   Having to do with the courts.

Foreseeable   Capable of being anticipated.

Forfeit   To lose, often as a consequence of an offense or a failure to perform some necessary act.

Forge   To fabricate a document by imitation with intent to commit fraud.

Forgery   The crime of falsely making or altering a document with intent to defraud.

Form   1. A model of a common legal paper.
2. The technical aspects of procedure (as opposed to the "substance" of a proceeding).

Fortuitous   Chance; unforeseen; accidental.

Forum   A court.

Forum non conveniens *(Latin)*   An inconvenient forum. If a court is so inconvenient as to be unjust to one or more of the participants, the case may, in the interests of justice, be moved elsewhere for trial.

Foundation   A basis; a support. A foundation must sometimes be laid before evidence can be admitted.

Four corners   What is actually written in a document. *See also* Face.

Franchise   A right that exists as a matter of law (such as the right to vote).

Fraud   Deceit or trickery used to deceive another.

Fraudulent   Done with intent to defraud.

Free   Without legal constraints.

Free on board *(F.O.B.)*   Loaded for shipment at no cost to buyer.

Freehold   An estate in real property either in fee or for life.

Frivolous   So inadequate as to be totally without merit.

Full faith and credit Total recognition. The Constitution requires that each state give full faith and credit to the judgments of its sister states.

Fungible Things that are identical and can therefore be substituted for each other, e.g., dollar bills.

Future interests An existing right to use property at some time in the future.

Futures Contracts for sale of commodities at a future date at a set price.

Gainful Profitable.

Garnish To notify; to warn; to summon. *Gọi đến liên toà*

Garnishee The person holding the property that is the subject of a garnishment.

Garnishment A process by which a creditor can collect a debt from a third party (the garnishee) who is holding the money or property of the debtor. *Khấu lương*

Gerrymander The changing of district lines in order to affect the political makeup of the district with the intention of benefiting a particular political party.

Gestation The period of the development of the fetus in the mother until the time of birth.

Gestum *(Roman law)* A deed; an act.

Gift A voluntary transfer of property without consideration or payment by the person receiving the gift.

Gift causa mortis A gift given in contemplation of death which takes effect on the death of the donor.

Good faith Fairness; honesty. *Thiện ý*

Goodwill The reputation of a business and the expectation that customers will continue to patronize it; the difference between the actual value of the business and the value of its physical assets.

Grand jury A jury that decides whether or not an accused is to be indicted.

Grandfather clause An exemption in a new law for people who are already engaged in the activity to be regulated.

Grant 1. (v) To give.
2. (n) The transfer of real property.

Grantee One who receives a grant.

Grantor One who grants.

Gratis Free; without consideration.

Gratuitous Without consideration; as a gift.

Gravamen *(Latin)* The essence, usually of a complaint.

Gross Great; flagrant; total.

Gross income Total money taken in before deduction of expenses.

Guaranty 1. A promise to perform the obligation of another should the other fail to perform.

2. A merchant's warranty that goods are of a certain quality.

Guardian A person who has custody and control of another who is not capable of taking care of himself, such as a minor or incompetent.

Guilty 1. (adj) Not innocent, convicted of a crime.

2. (n) The plea of a person who admits that the charge against him is true.

Habeas corpus *(Latin)* A writ which demands that a prisoner who is illegally held be brought into court so that the legality of the imprisonment may be determined.

Habendum *(Latin)* A clause in a deed that describes the extent of the estate being transferred.

Habitual By habit; customary.

Half-brother, half-sister Persons who have one parent in common.

Harassment A minor offense, including cursing, jostling, etc., with intent to bother another.

Harbor To shelter or give refuge to a person, particularly a person who is being sought by the police.

Hazard Danger or risk.

Hazardous Subject to hazard.

Hearing 1. A formal proceeding in which issues are tried.

2. A proceeding before an administrative agency.

Hearsay Evidence in the form of a written or oral statement by a person who is not available to testify at the actual trial and cannot, therefore, be cross-examined. It is offered as proof of what is asserted in the statement itself. Hearsay evidence is generally not admissible, although there exist many exceptions to this rule. The exceptions usually involve some set of facts that tends to make the evidence more believable, such as the fact that the statement in question was against the speaker's own interest at the time that it was made.

Heat of passion A violent emotional state, the existence of which may reduce to manslaughter a killing that would otherwise be murder.

Heir One who inherits property; one who inherits real property from an intestate.

Heir apparent One who would inherit real property from another should the other die intestate.

Heirs   Those who would inherit an estate in the case of an intestacy.

Heirs and assigns   Words used in the habendum clause to denote the passing of a fee simple.

Held   Decided (by a court).

Hereditary   Capable of being inherited.

Hire   To employ a person; to rent the use of some thing.

Hold   1. To decide.
     2. To own something.

Holder   A person in possession of a negotiable instrument.

Holder in due course   A holder who pays fair value for a negotiable instrument and has no reason to believe there is anything wrong with it. A person can be a holder in due course even if there is a defect in the instrument.

Holding company   A corporation that owns a controlling interest in at least one other corporation.

Holograph   A handwritten will, entirely in the handwriting of the person making the will.

Home   A dwelling place.

Homestead   A home, including the actual house and surrounding property. Some states protect the homestead from creditors.

Homicide   The culpable killing of a human being (it may or may not be a criminal act, depending on the circumstances).

Honor   To accept and pay, e.g., when a check is presented.

Honorarium   A gift or payment.

Hornbook   A legal textbook containing a review of the black letter law of a particular subject.

Hostile witness   A witness called by one party to a suit who so favors the other side that he can be cross-examined as if he or she were the other side's witness.

Hotchpot   The mixing together of property belonging to several individuals in order to divide it equally among them.

Housebreaking   Breaking into and entering a dwelling with the intent to commit a crime once inside. (If done at night, it is considered burglary.)

Household   People who live together as a family.

Hung jury   A jury that is unable to agree on a verdict.

Hypothesis   A supposition, theory, or assumption.

Hypothetical question   A question (which in court can only be asked of an expert witness) that assumes a set of facts and asks for an answer or an opinion based on the assumed facts.

I.C.C.   Interstate Commerce Commission.

I.E.   *See* Id est.

I.R.S.   Internal Revenue Service.

Ibidem *(Latin)*   In the same book or place. Abbreviated "ibid.".

Id est *(Latin)*   That is. Abbreviated "i.e.".

Idem *(Latin)*   The same.

Identity   Sameness.

Ignorance   Lack of knowledge.

Illegal   Against the law; unlawful.

Illegality   The state of being unlawful or illegal.

Illegitimate   Against the law; born to unmarried parents.

Illicit   Illegal; unlawful.

Illusory   Deceiving; e.g., an illusory promise is one in which the person making the promise is not actually bound to perform but can do so at his option.

Immediate   Present; not far away.

Immigration   Entry into a country by foreigners who intend to establish residence there.

Imminent   About to happen; impending. Imminent danger of death may justify a killing in self-defense.

Immunity   Exception contrary to the general rule, either from a duty or a penalty. Immunity from prosecution may be granted to certain witnesses.

Impair   To obstruct or make worse.

Impanel   To make a list of prospective jurors or to select the actual jury for a trial.

Impartial   Disinterested; not prejudiced.

Impeach   To accuse or discredit.

Impeachment   The discrediting of a person or of a witness; a trial to determine if a public officer should be removed from office for misconduct.

Impediment   A disability, obstruction, disqualification, or bar, e.g., to a marriage or to entrance into a contract.

Implead   To bring a new party into a lawsuit.

Implied   Understood, although not specifically stated.

Impossibility   That which is not possible. If a contract is impossible, it is not enforceable.

Impound   To hold in legal custody.

Imprisonment   The holding of a person; the exercise of restraint on personal liberty.

Improvement   A change for the better; an addition to real property that makes it more valuable.

Imputed   Charged to a person whether or not actually done by or known by that person (knowledge, negligence, income, and notice can all be imputed to a person in certain circumstances).

In loco parentis *(Latin)*   In the place of a parent.

In personam *(Latin)*   A suit brought to enforce rights against an individual. *See also* In rem.

In re *(Latin)*   In the matter of.

In rem *(Latin)*   A suit brought to enforce rights as to a particular piece of property. The rights thus established are valid against all persons. *See also* In personam.

In terrorem *(Latin)*   Literally, in threat; a clause in a will that revokes a gift to any person who contests the will for any reason.

In toto *(Latin)*   Completely.

Inadmissible   Things that cannot be allowed as evidence.

Incapacity   Legal or physical inability to do something.

Incarceration   Imprisonment.

Incest   Sexual intercourse between people who are close blood relatives (too close to marry legally).

Inchoate   Unfinished; incipient; incomplete.

Income   Monetary gain, especially from work and capital investments.

Income tax   A tax based on income.

Incompetency   Lack of some ability or legal right to perform some act; mental or physical incapacity. Incompetent evidence is evidence that is inadmissible.

Incorporate   To create a corporation.

Incriminate   To demonstrate or to make it appear that someone is guilty of a crime.

Incumber   *See* Encumber.

Indebtedness   The state of being in debt.

Indefeasible   Not able to be avoided or defeated.

Indemnify   To secure against loss or to reimburse for past loss.

Indemnity   A contract to secure another against a possible future loss.

Independent contractor   One who does work for another not as an employee, subject to the orders of the other, but under contract to be performed according to his own methods.

Indictment   A formal charge of the commission of a crime made by a grand jury after it hears testimony about the crime.

Indigent   Poor, needy.

Indorse   To write one's name on the back of a negotiable instrument (such as a check).

Indorsement   Signing a negotiable instrument on the back to authorize transfer to another person.

Inducement   Something that convinces a person to perform an act, enter into a deal, or sign a contract.

Infancy   A person who has not yet reached the age of majority, usually 18 years.

Inference   A deduction from known facts.

Information   1. A written accusation of a crime, a complaint.
2. A formal written accusation preferred by a prosecutor.
3. Acquired knowledge.

Information and belief   A qualifying statement, usually found in an affidavit, indicating that what follows is believed by the affiant to be true but is not necessarily offered as a fact.

Infra *(Latin)*   Below.

Infraction   A violation of a law, usually a minor law.

Infringement   An encroachment; a violation of some right (such as a copyright or patent).

Inherent   Intrinsic; inseparable from the thing itself.

Inherently dangerous   An item or situation that is dangerous by its very nature.

Inherit   To take or receive property as a result of an intestacy.

Inheritance   1. (n) Property that is inherited.
2. (v) The taking of property as a result of an intestacy or by descent. Also sometimes used to describe taking by will.

Injunction   The order of a court that a person either perform an act or refrain from some course of conduct.

Injury   The violation of some legal right of a person. Sometimes used to describe the resultant damage to the person.

Innocent   Not guilty, having done no wrong.

Inquest   A coroner's investigation into the cause of a death.

Insanity   The condition of having an unsound or deranged mind to the extent that one is unable to cope with ordinary situations. As a defense in a criminal action, it means that the defendant is incapable of having the intent to commit the crime or that he cannot distinguish right from wrong.

Insolvency   The state of having insufficient assets to pay one's debts.

Inspection   Careful examination.

Instant   Present; this one; current.

Insubordination   Refusal to obey orders or instructions.

Insurable interest   A person's real interest in the item or person to be insured. Without a real financial interest, there can be no valid insurance contract—it would merely be a wager.

Insurance   A contract under which one party agrees to indemnify the other against loss or liability resulting from some event (such as death, an automobile accident, or a fire).

Intangible assets   *(Intangibles)*   Incorporeal items; things with value but no physical substance; rights such as debts, owed to persons or bank accounts.

Intent   Determination to achieve a particular end by a particular means.

Inter *(Latin)*   Between.

Inter alia *(Latin)*   Among other things.

Inter vivos *(Latin)*   Between the living; an inter vivos gift is a gift made between living people (as opposed to a gift by will).

Interest   Any right in something; compensation payed by debtors to creditors for the use of money belonging to the latter.

Interim *(Latin)*   Temporary, in the meantime.

Interlocutory   A judgment by a court in a matter related to or part of the main case; an intermediate decision, but not the decision of the case itself.

Interloper   Someone who enters or interferes where he has no right to be.

Interpleader   A procedure under which a person holding money that may belong to one of several other parties may force all of the parties into court in order to determine who is entitled to the money.

Interpretation   The act of determining what is meant by a set of written words.

Interrogatories   Questions, usually written, asked of a witness, generally during the discovery procedure.

Interstate   Between two or more states.

Intervention   The voluntary appearance of a new party in a lawsuit, with the permission of the court.

Intestacy   The status of one who has died without having left a will.

Intestate   Without having made a will.

Intra *(Latin)*   Within.

Intrastate Within the state.

Inure To take effect.

Invalid Inadequate; having no effect; null and void.

Involuntary Unintentional.

Ipse dixit *(Latin)* He himself spoke.

Ipso facto *(Latin)* By the fact itself.

Irregularity A failure to follow proper procedure.

Issue 1. (v) To send forth.
    2. (n) The descendants of a person (children, grandchildren).
    3. (n) An item of contention.

J. Judge, justice.

J.D. Juris Doctor, the basic law degree.

J.P. *See* Justice of the peace.

Jeopardy Danger; the risk of being punished when one is on trial in a criminal case.

John Doe A fictitious name used in hypothetical situations or when a party's real name is not known.

Joinder Joining together. Parties can be joined (e.g., two parties can unite as plaintiffs in a case); causes of action can be joined if a party has two or more separate causes against the same defendant and wishes to try them together.

Joint United; combined.

Joint and several Both together and separately. If liability is joint and several, money can be collected from the group or any individual member.

Joint enterprise The engagement in some activity by two or more persons with a common interest or goal. Persons acting together with equal control toward the same purpose are said to be engaged in joint enterprise, and the negligence of one may be imputed to the other.

Joint venture A short-term joint enterprise in business.

Judge A public official who presides over a court of justice.

Judgment The final determination by a court in a proceeding before it.

Judgment-proof A person against whom a judgment for money is useless because the person is unable to pay or is somehow protected from paying.

Judicial Having to do with justice or with a judge.

Judicial notice The recognition by a judge that certain commonly known and indisputable facts are true even though they have not been presented as evidence.

Judicial review 1. The power of the courts to declare acts of the legislature unconstitutional.

2. The actual process of using that power.

Judiciary The branch of government that interprets the law and administers justice through a system of courts.

Jurisdiction The right of a court to exercise its power over a particular person or type of case.

Jurisdictional Necessary for jurisdiction. In some courts a minimum jurisdictional amount (of money) must be at stake before a case will be heard.

Jurisprudence The study of the law.

Jurist An expert in the law.

Juror A member of a jury.

Jury A group of laypersons who are selected to hear the facts and render an impartial verdict as to what is the truth. A grand jury determines whether the evidence justifies an indictment in a criminal case; a petit jury determines issues of fact in a trial.

Jus *(Latin)* Law; right.

Jus tertii *(Latin)* The right of a third party.

Just Fair; legal.

Justice 1. The fair treatment under the law sought to be achieved by the courts.

2. A judge of a superior court.

Justice of the peace A minor local judge.

Justiciable Appropriate for being tried in court.

Justification A valid reason for doing something that would otherwise be illegal.

Juxtaposition Placing side by side.

K.B. King's Bench, an English common law court.

Kidnapping Movement or imprisonment of a person against that person's will. Under early common law, the person had to be moved across county lines.

Kin Blood relatives.

Kleptomania An irresistible urge to steal.

Labor Work.

Labor dispute A controversy between employer and employees regarding some aspect or aspects of the terms of employment, e.g., salary, hours, benefits.

Labor union An association of employees formed for the purpose of bargaining with the employer.

Laches An equitable doctrine that prevents a person from winning a claim if he has delayed too long in pursuing it.

Landlord A person who leases land to another.

Lapse 1. Forfeiture of some right or privilege caused by a failure to perform a necessary act within a time limit.
2. The failure of a gift by will, causing the subject of the gift to go back into the residual estate. One common cause of failure is the death of the intended recipient occurring before the death of the testator.

Larceny Stealing, wrongfully taking. Grand larceny involves stealing more than a certain amount set by law; petit larceny less than that amount.

Lascivious Lewd; lustful.

Last clear chance The principle that a negligent plaintiff may recover for his injuries despite his negligence if the defendant could have avoided the damage after recognizing the danger (i.e., if the defendant had the "last clear chance" to avoid the accident).

Last in, first out *(LIFO)* A method of calculating the value of inventory, wherein items sold from stock are always considered to be those most recently obtained.

Latent Hidden; concealed.

Law 1. The entire set of rules which a government promulgates to regulate the behavior of the population.
2. Any individual statute enacted by the legislature.

Lawful Legal.

Lawyer A person licensed to practice law; an attorney.

Lay Not of the profession.

Layman A nonmember of the profession.

Leading case An important case deciding a particular point of law and looked upon by courts and counsel as a guide in future cases.

Leading question A question that suggests to the witness what answer the questioner wants.

Lease A contract for the rental of real property, creating a landlord–tenant relationship.

Leasehold The estate of a person who occupies real property by lease.

Ledger An account book.

Legacy A gift by will of personal property.

Legal According to law.

Legal age   The age of majority, usually 18, at which a person becomes able to make a contract.

Legatee   A person who receives a gift by will.

Legislate   To enact a law.

Legislation   1. The process of enacting laws.
2. The laws enacted by a legislative body.

Legislative   Referring to the branch of government that enacts laws; having to do with making laws.

Lessee   A person who rents property from another; a tenant.

Lessor   A person who rents property to another; a landlord.

Letters testamentary   The notice of official appointment of an executor by the court.

Levy   1. (v) To assess or collect (as a tax).
2. (n) A seizure.

Lex *(Latin)*   Law.

Lex loci *(Latin)*   The law of the place.

Lex loci contractus *(Latin)*   The law of the place of the contract.

Lex loci delictus *(Latin)*   The law of the place of the crime.

Liability   Legal responsibility.

Liable   Responsible.

Libel   A written defamation; a false statement in writing which causes some injury. If a statement is libelous per se, one need not prove any damage; if libelous per quod, the injurious effect of the statement must be proved.

Liberty   Freedom; absence of restraint.

License   1. A privilege to engage in a particular activity.
2. Unrestrained activity.

Licensee   1. A person who has a license.
2. A person who enters the property of another with permission, but to accomplish his own purposes rather than at the invitation of the owner.

Licentiousness   Self-indulgence; lewdness.

Lien   A claim against property as a result of some legal obligation of the owner; e.g., a mechanic may have a lien on property he has repaired.

Lien creditor   A person who has a lien on property as a result of a debt that is owed to him.

Life estate   An interest in property that lasts until the death of the holder of the life estate or some other person.

Life tenant   The holder of a life estate.

LIFO   *See* Last in, first out.

Limit   1. (v) To restrain.
2. (n) A restraint.

Limitation   A restriction.

Limited   Restricted.

Limited liability   The liability of owners of a corporation. They are liable only to the extent of their investments in the corporation, not their personal wealth.

Liquidate   To pay a debt.

Liquidated   Paid; fixed. Liquidated damages are a sum determined in advance by parties to a contract as the damages that will have to be paid in the event of a breach.

Liquidation   1. The settlement of a debt.
2. The winding up of a company.

Lis *(Latin)*   A suit or dispute.

Lis pendens *(Latin)*   A pending suit.

Litigant   A person engaged in a lawsuit.

Litigate   To carry on a lawsuit.

Litigation   A lawsuit.

Local   Relating to a particular place.

Local action   An action that can be brought only in one jurisdiction, the place where it arose.

Lockout   The employer's equivalent of a strike; a refusal to allow employees to come to work.

Locus *(Latin)*   A place or location.

Long-arm statute   A law that extends the jurisdiction of a state's courts in certain cases to people outside of the state.

Loss   Damage.

Lot   1. A piece of land.
2. A collected group of items.

Magistrate   A minor judge or justice of the peace.

Maim   To mutilate.

Major   A person who has reached the age, usually 18, where he is allowed to make contracts (the age of majority).

Majority   Legal age.

Malefactor   A criminal.

Malfeasance   Wrongdoing.

Malice Ill will.

Malice aforethought Premeditated malice.

Malicious Motivated by malice, e.g., malicious injury is prompted by ill will toward the person injured; malicious mischief is willful destruction of property; malicious prosecution is brought without just cause but only to harass the defendant.

Malpractice Incompetence or misconduct by a professional, usually a doctor or a lawyer.

Malum *(Latin)* Bad; wrong.

Malum in se *(Latin)* Inherently wrong, involving moral turpitude.

Malum prohibitum *(Latin)* Wrong because it is forbidden by law; not involving moral turpitude.

Mandamus *(Latin)* Literally, we command. An order of a court that directs some government official to do something.

Mandate A command issued by a court.

Mandatory Obligatory; imperative.

Manifest Obvious; evident.

Manslaughter Unlawful homicide, either voluntarily or involuntarily, but without malice.

Manumission 1. Liberation from slavery or servitude.
2. Emancipation of a child from its parents.

Marital Having to do with marriage.

Maritime Having to do with the sea.

Market A place set aside for buying and selling.

Market price *See* Fair market value.

Marketable Salable.

Marketable title Good, clear title to land.

Marshal A federal court officer whose duties, like those of a sheriff, include serving process, etc.

Marshal evidence A review of the evidence by the judge during his charge to the jury.

Martial law Military government.

Master 1. A special court official.
2. An employer.

Material Germane; important: e.g., a material fact is crucial to a case.

Material witness A key witness in a criminal case, whose testimony is so important that he may be incarcerated until the trial.

Materialman A person who supplies materials for a construction job.

Matrimonial Pertaining to marriage.

Matrimony Marriage.

Mechanic A skilled workman.

Mechanic's lien A workman's claim against the property he has worked on—he may hold onto the property until he has been paid.

Mediation Settlement of disputes by arbitration or intervention of a third party who seeks to reconcile the disputing parties.

Meeting of minds Agreement by the parties to a contract as to the purpose and terms of the contract.

Memorandum 1. A brief submitted to argue a point of law.
2. An informal writing.

Menacing A statutory offense much like common law assault, in which the victim is placed in fear of physical harm.

Mens rea *(Latin)* Guilty mind; wrongful intent.

Mental anguish Grief; mental suffering.

Mercantile Commercial; having to do with business.

Merchant A retailer.

Merchantable Of salable quality, suitable for the purpose for which it was purchased.

Merger Joining of two or more separate things, e.g., corporations.

Merits The substantive issues of a case (as opposed to procedural issues).

Minor An infant under the age of contractual capacity (usually 18).

Minority The status of an infant (a child under the age of 18).

Miranda rule The rule that a prisoner must receive certain warnings before he can be questioned by the police (e.g., he has the right to remain silent and to have a lawyer present).

Miscegenation Intermarriage between persons of different races.

Misdemeanor A crime of less gravity than a felony.

Misfeasance Wrongdoing.

Misrepresentation A false statement.

Mistake An error or an unintentional act.

Mistrial A trial that ends as a nullity due to some error that occurs during its course. The jury must be dismissed and a new jury selected.

Mitigate To lessen in degree or severity, e.g., a mitigating circumstance may lower the punishment for a crime.

M'naghten rule A test to determine whether a person can be held responsible for a criminal act. The determining factor is whether the person was able to distinguish right from wrong at the time of the act.

Modus *(Latin)* Method.

Modus operandi *(Latin)* Method of operation. Abbreviated M.O.

Monopoly Unilateral control of some market or the sole right to sell or do some particular thing.

Moot Abstract; hypothetical; academic.

Moot court A make-believe court in which students practice arguing cases.

Moral turpitude Vile and immoral behavior; depravity.

Mortgage A contract under which real estate (or personal property in the case of a chattel mortgage) is used as security for a loan.

Mortgagee The lender in a mortgage contract.

Mortgagor The borrower in a mortgage contract.

Mortis causa *(Latin)* Because of death.

Motion An application to a judge for a ruling on some point in a case.

Movant A person who makes a motion.

Move To make a motion.

Moving papers Papers filed in support of a motion.

Mulct A penalty or a fine.

Municipal Having to do with local government or the government of a town or city.

Municipal corporation An incorporated city or town.

Municipality A municipal corporation.

Murder An unlawful homicide, committed with malice aforethought or deliberate intent and no justification. *See also* Felony murder rule.

Mutatis mutandis *(Latin)* With the necessary changes.

Mutual Common to both parties; the same for both parties.

Mutuality Reciprocating; the state of being mutual.

N.B. *See* Nota bene.

N.L.R.B. National Labor Relations Board.

N.O.V. *See* Non obstante veredicto.

Natural law Laws that are basic to the nature of man; principles that are thought to be universal among civilized people.

Naturalization The granting of citizenship to a foreigner.

Neglect Failure to perform some legal obligation.

Negligence The failure to exercise proper care or due diligence.

Negligent Careless; exhibiting negligence.

Negotiable instrument A written and signed instrument (document), absolutely promising to pay to order or to bearer a specific sum of money at a specific time or on demand.

Negotiate 1. To transfer a negotiable instrument.
         2. To reach a compromise or an agreement; to make a deal.

Nemo *(Latin)* No one.

Net Total that remains after expenses and other deductions.

Next friend A person who acts for an infant in a lawsuit when the infant's parent or guardian is not available.

Next of kin A person's closest blood relatives.

Nexus Link; connection.

Nihil, nil *(Latin)* Nothing.

Nisi *(Latin)* Unless.   *Decree Nisi*

Nisi prius *(Latin)* Literally, unless before. A trial court.

Nolle prosequi *(Latin)* Formal declaration by a prosecutor that he will not prosecute a case.

Nolo contendere *(Latin)* Literally, I will not contend; equivalent to a plea of guilty.

Nomen *(Latin)* Name.

Nominal In name only.

Non *(Latin)* Not.

Non compos mentis *(Latin)* Mentally incompetent; insane; not of sound mind.

Non obstante veredicto *(Latin)* Notwithstanding verdict. A judge may, if he finds that the law requires it, reverse the jury's verdict in favor of one side and award judgment to the other side.

Nonfeasance Failure to meet some obligation.

Nonsuit A judgment against plaintiff because he has failed to take some necessary action.

Not guilty Innocent. The plea of a person who does not admit guilt when accused of a crime.

Nota bene *(Latin)* Note well. Abbreviated N.B. or n.b.

Notary public Public official who is able to certify documents and administer oaths.

Note A promise (in writing) to pay a specific sum of money at a specific time.

Notice Information; knowledge. Actual notice is actual knowledge; constructive notice means the person should have known, and the knowledge is charged to him.

Novation The substitution of a new contract for an old one.

Noxious Harmful.

Nugatory Invalid or ineffective.

Nuisance   Something that causes harm or inconvenience to another.

Null   Void; having no effect.

Nullity   Something that is null.

Nunc pro tunc *(Latin)*   Literally, now for then. Something that has retroactive effect.

Nuncupative will   An oral will.

Nuptial   Having to do with marriage.

Oath   Formal promise to tell the truth or to perform some act.

Obiter *(Latin)*   Incidentally.

Obiter dictum *(Latin)*   Unnecessary words in an opinion. *See also* Dictum.

Object   To protest or raise an objection.

Objection   A statement of protest or opposition to some statement or
action by the other side in a lawsuit on the grounds that it is in some
way improper.

Obligation   A duty that arises out of a contract, promise, or debt.

Obligee   A person to whom an obligation is owed.

Obligor   A person who incurs an obligation.

Obscene   Offensive, such as being lewd or indecent.

Obstruct   To impede or hinder.

Obstructing justice   The crime of interfering with justice, e.g., by hiding
evidence or keeping a witness from reaching court.

Occupancy   Possession of real property.

Occupant   Person in possession of real property.

Occupation   1. Possession of real property.
2. One's profession.

Offense   A violation of the criminal law.

Offer   1. A presentation or proposal of terms for a contract or deal.
2. A presentation of possible evidence.

Officer of the court   A general term for persons responsible to the court,
including judges, clerks, other official employees, and attorneys.

Officers   The persons who fill the offices created by the by-laws of a
corporation (president, secretary, etc.).

Official   1. (adj) Pertaining to an office, formal.
2. (n)   A person who occupies an authoritative position.

Omnibus *(Latin)*   1. (n)   Everything.
2. (adj)   Containing more than one item.

Onus *(Latin)*   Burden.

Open   To begin.

Opening statement A statement that the opposing lawyers may make, on the record, at the start of the trial. In it they outline what they plan to demonstrate with the evidence they will present.

Opinion The court's statement which announces and explains the court's decision.

Option An agreement in which, in exchange for some consideration, one person agrees to sell something to another at a specified price if the second party wishes to buy within a certain time period.

Oral Spoken.

Order A command; a written demand for payment of money to a third person.

Ordinance A law enacted by a municipality.

Overdraft A check written for a larger amount of money than is in the account upon which it is drawn.

Overrule To deny; to declare an earlier ruling or precedent no longer valid and replace it with a different decision.

Overt Open; public.

Ownership The rights of an owner to possess and control property.

P. Abbreviation for page.

Palpable Obvious, clear.

Par Equal; same.

Par value Face value.

Paralegal A person who is not a lawyer but has some legal training and works assisting lawyers.

Parcel A piece of real estate.

Pardon Forgiveness granted by the sovereign or highest executive (president or governor) exempting a person from punishment for a crime.

Parens patriae *(Latin)* The right of the government to care for those who are not competent to care for themselves.

Parity Equality.

Parol Oral; verbal.

Parol evidence Oral evidence; evidence not in writing. The parol evidence rule prevents the consideration of oral evidence to modify a written contract.

Parole Early release from a prison sentence provided that the convict abides by certain conditions placed upon him at the time of his release.

Particulars Items of an account; details of a claim.

Partition   Division of property belonging to co-owners into smaller pieces to be owned by each individually.

Partner   A member of a partnership.

Partnership   An association of two or more competent persons to be co-owners of a business for a profit.

Party   A person who is directly involved in a transaction or a lawsuit.

Passive   Inactive.

Passive negligence   Negligence resulting from a failure to act.

Patent   1. (adj)   Evident, obvious.
2. (n)   The exclusive right, guaranteed by the government of an inventor, to produce and sell an invention.
3. (n)   A government grant of land.

Paternity   The state of fatherhood.

Pauper   A poor person; a person receiving governmental support.

Pay   To discharge a debt.

Payee   A person who is designated on a negotiable instrument as the person to whom payment is to be made; a person to whom payment is made.

Payment   The discharge of a debt or obligation by the transfer of money or the equivalent.

Payor   A person who makes payment or is designated on a negotiable instrument as the person by whom payment is to be made.

Pecuniary   Having to do with money.

Pedigree   Ancestry or lineage.

Peers   Equals.

Penal   Punishable; having to do with punishment.

Penal law   The law relating to crimes and their punishments.

Penalty   A punishment brought about by operation of law.

Pendens *(Latin)*   Pending.

Pendent jurisdiction   The doctrine that allows federal courts to hear non-federal questions when they are related to federal questions properly before the court.

Pending   Begun but not yet finished.

People   The state.

Per *(Latin)*   By; through; by means of.

Per annum *(Latin)*   By the year.

Per autre vie *(French)*   For the lifetime of another.

Per capita *(Latin)*   By the head.

Per cent *(Latin)*   By the hundred.

Per curiam *(Latin)*   By the court. It denotes an opinion of the whole court as opposed to an opinion of a single judge.

Per diem *(Latin)*   By the day.

Per quod *(Latin)*   Whereby; because of its result.

Per se *(Latin)*   By itself.

Per stirpes *(Latin)*   Literally, by roots. Giving equally to each branch of the family rather than to each person, as in per capita.

Peremptory   Absolute; conclusive.

Perfect   To complete; to make complete, to execute.

Perfected   Completed; executed.

Performance   Complete fulfillment of a duty (such as a contractual obligation).

Perjury   Willful lying under oath.

Perpetrator   A person who actually commits a crime.

Perpetuity   A limitation on the use of property for a period longer than a life in being, plus 21 years. Such a limitation will not be enforced. (This is known as the rule against perpetuities.)

Person   An individual human being (a natural person) or a corporation (an artificial person).

Personal property   Movable property as opposed to real property.

Personalty   Personal property.

Petition   A formal written request or application.

Petitioner   One who presents a petition.

Picket   A person who takes part in picketing.

Picketing   The stationing of workers outside a place of business to promote a strike or boycott.

Plaintiff   A person who brings a suit or complaint against another.

Plea   The answer of a defendant to a criminal charge.

Plea bargaining   The process by which a defendant is given an opportunity to plead guilty to a lesser offense than the one with which he is charged, instead of going to trial.

Plead   To make a plea or file a pleading.

Pleading   A formal written statement of position submitted by each party to a case.

Pledge   The bailment (handing over) of personal property as security for a debt.

Plenary   Total; full; complete.

Plurality The greatest number of votes received by any candidate (even if not a majority or more than half of the total).

Police Governmental law enforcement agency.

Police power Generally, the power of the government to regulate the activities of the populace.

Political Having to do with the administration of government.

Polling the jury Asking each member of the jury to state his agreement with the verdict in a case.

Polygamy The illegal practice of having more than one spouse at a time.

Possess To occupy or control property; to have in one's physical control.

Possession Occupancy and control of property.

Post *(Latin)* After.

Post-mortem *(Latin)* After death.

Post-mortem examination Examination after death; more generally, an examination after any event.

Posthumous Occurring after death.

Power The right or ability to take some action.

Power of attorney A written instrument authorizing another to act as agent or attorney for the writer.

Practice 1. Custom or habit; procedure.
2. The engagement of a person in a profession.

Precatory Requesting (as opposed to demanding).

Precedent 1. An earlier judicial decision that has authoritative effect on a case to be decided.
2. Something that has already taken place.

Prefer 1. To prosecute.
2. To favor.

Preference The payment of one creditor before another.

Prejudice 1. A preconceived opinion; bias.
2. Detriment.

Prejudicial error Error that was detrimental enough to affect the result of a case.

Premeditation Forethought; planning.

Preponderance of evidence The greater weight of the evidence; the set of evidence that is more convincing.

Prerogative A privilege.

Prescription To obtain title to property by adverse possession. *See also* Adverse possession.

Presentment The presenting of a bill to the drawee for acceptance.

Presumption A rule that orders that a certain inference be drawn if a certain fact is ascertained.

Pretermitted heir A child or other legal heir left out of a will.

Prima facie *(Latin)* On its face.

Prima facie case A case in which enough evidence is presented to prove what is alleged unless the other side puts forth evidence to disprove it.

Primogeniture The system under which all real estate passes automatically on the death of the owner to his eldest son.

Principal
1. (adj) Primary.
2. (n) A person who is responsible for the acts done for his benefit by others appointed by him (his agents).
3. (n) A person who is directly involved in a crime.
4. (n) The body of a loan, which must be paid back together with interest that accrues.
5. (n) In suretyship, the original debtor.

Principle A general or fundamental truth.

Prior Previous; earlier.

Priority Precedence.

Privacy The basic right to be left alone.

Private Belonging to an individual or individuals.

Privilege A right that is not held by the public at large, but only by an individual or a group of individuals.

Privity
1. A direct financial relationship between the parties to a contract or a deal.
2. An identity of interest between people.

Privy
1. (n) A person who is in privity with another.
2. (adj) Private.

Pro *(Latin)* For.

Pro rata *(Latin)* Proportionately.

Pro se *(Latin)* For himself.

Probable cause Reasonable cause under the circumstances.

Probate The process of judging whether or not a will is valid.

Probation A period of being under observation for a length of time instead of being incarcerated after being convicted of a crime.

Probative Tending to prove something.

Procedure The rules of carrying on an action in court.

Proceeding A court case.

Proceeds Money or other valuable property received in exchange for something.

Process 1. The legal means of securing a defendant's appearance in court; a summons.

2. A method of doing something. *See also* Due process of law.

Profits Gains.

Prohibit To forbid.

Promise To bind oneself to do something.

Promisee A person to whom a promise is made.

Promissor A person who makes a promise.

Promissory note A written promise to pay a specific amount of money at a specific time.

Promoter A person involved in forming a corporation.

Proof The conclusive establishment of a fact by means of some evidence.

Proper Suitable; appropriate.

Property Anything that is capable of being owned, either personal (movable) property or real (land) property.

Proponent A person who offers or proffers something.

Proprietary Relating to ownership.

Prorate To divide on a pro rata basis; to distribute proportionately.

Prosecute To proceed against in court.

Prosecution A criminal proceeding.

Prosecutor A government official who prosecutes criminal cases.

Prospectus A description of property or corporate stock that is for sale.

Provisional Temporary.

Proviso A condition or restriction or a clause that imposes one.

Proximate Immediate; direct.

Proximate cause The cause that actually leads to an injury; the one event without which the injury could not have taken place.

Proxy A written authorization to one person to act for another.

Public Pertaining to the state or nation as opposed to individuals.

Publication Making known to the public, either orally or in writing.

Publish To make known to the public.

Punishment A penalty brought about by operation of law.

Punitive Having to do with punishment.

Purchase To buy.

Purport To appear on the surface.

Pursuant Consequential; in accordance with.

Putative Alleged; reputed.

Qua *(Latin)* As.

Quaere *(Latin)* Question, query.

Quantum meruit *(Latin)* What it is worth; what has been earned.

Quash Suppress or vacate; annul.

Quasi *(Latin)* As if; similar to.

Quasi in rem An action in which the rights of the parties are determined with regard to some particular property.

Query Question.

Quid pro quo *(Latin)* Literally, what for what, or something for something. The consideration underlying a contract.

Quiet enjoyment Legal, quiet, and peaceful possession of real property.

Quit To leave or vacate.

Quitclaim A deed giving up any claim of right that one might have regarding some property.

Quorum The number of members (usually a majority) of a body needed for the body to vote or conduct business.

Rape The crime of a man unlawfully forcing a woman to engage in sexual intercouse with him. *See also* Statutory rape.

Ratification Approval, acceptance, confirmation of, or giving effect to an act already performed.

Re *(Latin)* Concerning; relating to; in the matter of.

Real evidence Physical evidence or other evidence that can be sensed directly by the jury without relying on testimony.

Real property Land and other immovable property (such as buildings).

Realty Real property.

Reasonable Sensible; proper; usual.

Rebut To deny; to refute; to contradict.

Rebuttable Arguable; disputable.

Receipt Written acknowledgment that something, usually money, has been received.

Receiver The person who acts as custodian for property in receivership.

Receivership The placing of property into the hands of a court-appointed custodian (receiver) to ensure that it is managed properly.

Recidivist A habitual criminal.

Reciprocal Mutual.

Reciprocity Mutuality.

Reckless Extremely careless.

Reckless endangerment The offense of behaving in such a reckless manner as to place another in danger of serious injury.

Recognizance A formal obligation, entered into in court, to perform some act. A prisoner may be released on his own recognizance in lieu of posting of bail.

Recompense Payment; reward; remuneration.

Record 1. (v) To make an official notation; to enter in writing.
        2. (n) A written account of some proceeding.

Recorder An official in charge of public records.

Recording act A statute that regulates the recording of certain documents, usually deeds and other instruments involving real estate.

Recoupment Holding back something from another party as a setoff for what the other party owes you; recovering lost money.

Recovery The amount that the plaintiff is awarded on winning a lawsuit.

Redeem To recover or buy back.

Redeemable Subject to redemption.

Redemption A recovery or buying back of property.

Referee A person appointed by a court to try certain issues.

Referee in bankruptcy A federal judge who hears bankruptcy cases.

Register 1. (n) An official record.
        2. (v) To record.

Registrar A person who keeps records in a register.

Regular Lawful; proper.

Regulate To control or place restrictions but not prohibit.

Release Abandonment of some claim against another.

Relevancy Logical nexus between evidence and what is to be demonstrated by the evidence.

Relevant Relating to the issue at hand in such a way as to be helpful in determining the truth about the issue.

Relief The remedy granted by a court, be it money, damages, injunction, etc.

Remainder An interest in property that takes effect only on the expiration of the interest previously in effect (e.g., "estate to A for life, remainder to B" means that B's interest takes effect when A dies).

Remainderman A person who is entitled to a remainder.

Remand To return or send back. A higher court may remand a case to the lower court from which it came for a new trial or further proceedings.

Remedial Corrective, relating to a remedy.

Remedy What is done to compensate for an injury or to enforce some right.

Remit To send; to pay.

Removal The transfer or movement, either of a person from one place to another, or of a case from one court to another.

Render To yield or deliver.

Rent 1. (n) The compensation paid for the use of real estate.
2. (v) To let real property.

Renvoi *(French)* A returning or sending back. In conflicts of laws cases, a repudiated doctrine that led to a never-ending cycle in trying to determine which forum's law was applicable to a particular case.

Repeal To end the effect of one law through the passing of another.

Replevin *(French)* An action to recover property unlawfully taken.

Reply An additional pleading by a plaintiff in response to defendant's answer. Not all cases call for a reply.

Report An official record of a proceeding.

Reporter A person who is charged with recording the proceedings of a court.

Represent 1. To assert.
2. To act for.

Representation 1. An assertion of fact (whether or not it is true).
2. Acting for another, e.g., as a lawyer acting for a client.

Representative One who acts for another.

Reprieve A temporary postponement of the carrying out of a sentence.

Republication A reinstatement of a will which had been revoked but not destroyed at some earlier time.

Repudiate To reject; to deny.

Repudiation Rejection; refusal to accept as valid.

Res *(Latin)* The thing.

Res gestae *(Latin)* Literally, things done. The entire event. Evidence may be excepted from the usual prohibition against hearsay if it is part of the res gestae of a case, i.e., if it is part of the whole occurrence.

Res ipsa loquitur *(Latin)* Literally, the thing itself speaks. When a person had control immediately before an accident of the thing that caused the accident, the person is presumed responsible. The person thus held responsible may, of course, offer evidence to the contrary.

Res judicata *(Latin)* Literally, the thing already adjudicated or decided. Once a question is decided between two litigants, they cannot bring another suit to determine the same question.

Rescind To bring about a rescission.

Rescission Annulment of a contract either by agreement or judicial order.

Residence The place where a person lives.

Residuary That which is left over.

Residuary estate The part of the estate that is left over when the specific gifts have been paid.

Respondeat superior *(Latin)* Literally, the master answers. The doctrine that establishes an employer's liability for acts of his employees done in furtherance of their employment.

Respondent 1. The person who answers an appeal.
  2. The winner in a lower court against whom an appeal is taken; the appellee.

Restitution The paying back or restoration to a person who has been deprived of what was rightfully his.

Restraining order An injunction.

Restraint of trade Illegal interference with normal competition.

Retainer Preliminary fee given to a lawyer at the time he is officially engaged.

Retract To take back, e.g., to retract an offer.

Retraction The withdrawal of an earlier statement.

Retroactive Relating to what has already taken place.

Retrospective Retroactive; looking backward.

Reus *(Latin)* A defendant, criminal, or party to an action.

Revenue Income; profit.

Reversal The setting aside of what has been done and, usually, substitution of the opposite.

Reverse To set aside; e.g., an appellate court can reverse the decision of a lower court.

Reversion A future interest in real property held by a person who transfers the property to another. It takes effect at the end of the other party's estate.

Revert To return to.

Review A reconsideration of a case at the appellate level.

Revival A restoration.

Revocation A taking back; nullification; cancellation.

Revoke   To nullify or cancel.

Right   1. (adj)   Proper; legal; correct.
2. (n)   Something to which a person is entitled, be it a thing or a privilege.

Riot   A tumultuous breach of the peace by three or more people.

Riparian   Having to do with the bank of a river.

Robbery   Taking of property from another against his will by force or threat of force.

Rule   1. (v)   To decide an issue.
2. (n)   A regulation.

Ruling   A decision on a question during a trial.

Running with the land   An agreement that binds any owner of the land, present or future.

S.C.   Supreme Court.

S.E.C.   Securities and Exchange Commission.

Said   Previously mentioned.

Salable   Capable of being sold.

Sale   A transfer of ownership of property in return for payment or a contract to pay.

Salvage   The property recovered from the remains of an accident or disaster.

Sanction   1. Approval.
2. A penalty imposed by law.

Satisfaction   Final discharge of an obligation.

Scienter   *(Latin)*   Knowledge, especially guilty knowledge.

Scintilla   *(Latin)*   A tiny bit.

Scrivener   A writer or scribe.

Seal   An official symbol on a document signifying authenticity.

Sealed   Authenticated by a seal.

Sealed verdict   A verdict reached by jury after court is adjourned. It is sealed in an envelope and read at the next session.

Search   An examination or investigation involving an intrusion into the privacy of the subject.

Search and seizure   The discovery and confiscation by law enforcement officials of property belonging to a suspected criminal.

Search warrant   A written authorization from a judge or magistrate allowing the police, upon a showing of probable cause, to search a designated area for specific evidence of a crime.

Secondary boycott   Indirect pressure on a business by boycotting other businesses that deal with it.

Secular   Not pertaining to religion or spiritual things; worldly.

Secure   To guarantee payment with some collateral or security.

Secured creditor   A creditor in a transaction where the debt is guaranteed with some security.

Secured transaction   An obligation secured by a property interest.

Securities   Instruments, such as stocks or bonds, sold publicly by a company.

Security   Property in which a debtor gives a creditor some interest in order to guarantee payment of the debt.

Sedition   A verbal or written attempt to incite resistance to the government.

Seisin   *(French)*   Possession in fee of land by the owner.

Seizure   The forcible taking of a person or thing. *See also* Search and seizure.

Self-defense   The use of force to protect oneself or others from harm.

Seller   The party who transfers property in a contract of sale.

Sentence   The judgment of a criminal court as to what punishment shall be inflicted upon a convicted defendant.

Sequester   1. (n) The seizing of property by a court to guarantee obedience of the court's decree.
2. (v) To isolate a jury during its deliberations to prevent contact with outside influences.

Servant   An employee.

Service   The delivery or other communication of notice of a lawsuit or other legal papers to the opposing party.

Servient   Under servitude to another. For example, a servient estate is an estate in land under an easement that benefits another estate.

Servitude   1. An easement; a burden on an estate.
2. The state of being a servant or a slave.

Session   A sitting of a court or a legislature.

Setoff   A claim by a defendant against the plaintiff based on an unrelated basis but which would, if proven, reduce the amount plaintiff can recover from defendant.

Settle   1. To reach an agreement about disposition of a pending suit or other claim of one person against another.
2. To establish a trust.

Settlor   A person who establishes a trust.

Several More than two; separate and distinct.

Sewer service The throwing away of a paper that was to have been served on a party and then claiming that it was, in fact, properly delivered.

Sham Fake, false.

Share 1. Part of an estate.
2. A unit of corporate stock.

Shareholder *See* Stockholder.

Shelley's case The rule in Shelley's case, no longer in effect in most jurisdictions, held that if a life estate were granted with the remainder granted to the grantee's heirs, the grantee would be awarded an estate in fee.

Sheriff A public official who serves as a peace officer and is responsible for serving process in various civil and criminal actions.

Short sale A contract of sale of securities that the seller does not own but borrows, usually from his broker, with the intention of replacing in the near future.

Show cause order An order by a court to a party before it to offer reasons why the court should not take action that an opposing party has requested.

Shyster A shady or dishonest lawyer or businessman.

Sic *(Latin)* Literally, so, in this manner. Used in citing a quotation containing an error to indicate that the error was in the original material.

Sign To affix one's signature.

Signature A person's name, on any instrument or document, affixed by himself, with the intent to authorize the instrument or document.

Sine qua non *(Latin)* Literally, without which is not. Something that is indispensable.

Site A specific place used or intended to be used for a specific purpose.

Situs *(Latin)* Location.

Slander Oral defamation; words spoken falsely with intention to injure another.

Slander per se Slander in and of itself, actionable even without a showing of damage to plaintiff (e.g., false statement that a person has committed a crime of moral turpitude or has a loathsome disease).

Small claims court A court that has jurisdiction over claims that do not exceed a certain sum (usually $500 to $1,000), providing a brief, simple, and inexpensive proceeding, and where a person can sue without engaging an attorney.

Sodomy Deviate intercourse; any unnatural sex act.

Solicit To entreat, ask for, or entice.

Solicitor *(English)* An attorney.

Solvency The state of being solvent.

Solvent Able to pay one's debts as they come due.

Special appearance Appearing in court solely to argue that the court has no jurisdiction over one's person.

Specie Coin made of gold or silver.

Specific performance The compelling (by a court) of a party to a contract to do what the contract requires.

Speedy trial A trial free from excessive delays, a right of every accused.

Spendthrift A free or careless spender.

Spendthrift trust A trust created to provide for a person and to prevent the beneficiary from dissipating the fund unwisely or too quickly.

Spoliation 1. Plundering.
2. Material alteration of an instrument by a person not a party to the instrument.

Standing to sue Capacity to bring an action because one's interest in the outcome is direct.

Stare decisis *(Latin)* Literally, the decision should stand. The doctrine that gives authority to prior decisions of a court and makes courts reluctant to reverse their prior decisions.

Statement A declaration or allegation.

State's evidence Testimony of a witness who was involved in a crime but is granted leniency in return for his testimony.

Status Condition or position.

Status quo *(Latin)* The existing state of things.

Statute A law enacted by the legislature.

Statute of limitations A law setting forth the respective periods of time within which various actions may be brought.

Statutory rape Intercourse with a female younger than a certain age, regardless of whether she consents.

Stay 1. (v) To stop or postpone.
2. (n) A postponement.

Stipend A periodic payment; a salary.

Stipulate To agree; to concede.

Stipulation An agreement made by the attorneys on opposite sides regarding some matter in a lawsuit.

Stock 1. Certificates of ownership in a corporation.
     2. Goods held for sale by a merchant.

Stockholder A person who owns shares of corporate stock.

Strict Precise; exact.

Strict construction Very literal or narrow reading of a statute.

Strict liability Absolute responsibility for damage, even in the absence of a showing of negligence.

Strike 1. (n) A work stoppage by employees involved in a dispute with the employer.
     2. (v) To expunge; remove.

Sua sponte *(Latin)* On his own.

Sub judice *(Latin)* Under judicial consideration; as yet undecided.

Subject matter jurisdiction The power of the court to hear a particular type of case.

Suborn To procure an unlawful act.

Subpoena A court order that a person appear in court.

Subpoena duces tecum A subpoena ordering a person not only to appear but also to bring some evidence with him.

Subrogation The substitution of one person for another in a claim against a third party. The person who is substituted is entitled to all the rights of the original party.

Subscribe To sign at the end of a document.

Substantial Material; real; significant; valuable.

Substantive The part of the law that regulates rights (as opposed to procedural law, which regulates enforcement).

Succession The transfer of property to legal heirs when a person dies intestate.

Sue To institute a lawsuit.

Sufference Toleration.

Suffrage The right to vote.

Sui generis *(Latin)* Unique; of its own kind.

Sui juris *(Latin)* In his own right; having capacity.

Suit A legal action; a lawsuit.

Summary Short; immediate; abbreviated; concise.

Summary judgment A judgment rendered when the evidence offered by defendant is patently insufficient to controvert plaintiff's case.

Summation Concluding argument of a lawyer after the last testimony and before the judge charges the jury.

Summons The writ that informs a defendant of the existence of the case. A summons, when it is properly served, commences a proceeding.

Superior Higher.

Supersede To set aside and replace.

Supervene To intervene or interpose.

Supplemental Additional; added to make the original complete.

Suppress 1. To prohibit or restrain.
2. To keep out of evidence.

Supra (Latin) Above; earlier.

Sur *(French)* On; upon.

Surety A person who enters a contract of suretyship.

Suretyship An arrangement under which one party agrees to guaranty the payment of the debt of another.

Surrogate 1. A judge in charge of probate of wills.
2. One who acts in place of another.

Sustain To uphold; to grant.

Swear To administer an oath.

Sworn Under oath; verified.

Synod A meeting of church officials.

T.R.O. *See* Temporary restraining order.

Tacit Implied.

Tail Limited, usually to issue (children, grandchildren, etc.).

Tangible Real; tactile; subject to physical possession and being touched.

Tax A forced contribution to the government, based on some reasonable system of apportionment of the burden.

Taxable income That part of the income (after deductions and exemptions, etc.) upon which the income tax is computed.

Temporary restraining order A temporary injunction; an order of a court that is issued to curb some activity until a full hearing can be held.

Tenancy The estate, or occupancy, of a tenant.

Tenant One who occupies real property owned by another, under some understanding with the owner.

Tender Offer of payment coupled with the intention and the ability to deliver.

Terra *(Latin)* Land; earth.

Test case A suit brought for the specific purpose of litigating a particular point in order to determine the law establishing a particular right.

Testacy   The state of dying leaving a valid will.

Testament   A will.

Testamentary   Having to do with a will.

Testate   A person who dies leaving a will.

Testator   A person who makes a will.

Testify   To give evidence under oath.

Testimony   The evidence given by a witness in a case.

Third party   A person not a party to the original transaction (contract, lawsuit, etc.) but who might be connected indirectly or brought in in some way.

Third party beneficiary   The beneficiary of a contract made by two other parties.

Time is of the essence   A condition in a contract that makes it a material breach to fail to perform within the time specified.

Title   Estate in fee; absolute ownership of real property.

Toll   1. (v) To suspend or put off the running of a statute of limitation.
2. (n) A fee for use of a public road or bridge.

Tort   A wrong or injury inflicted on another as a result of a breach of an existing legal duty.

Tortfeasor   One who commits a tort.

Tortious   Wrongful.

Totten trust   A trust consisting of a bank account deposited by one person in his own name in trust for another. It is generally revocable at the will of the depositor, but passes to the beneficiary at his death.

Tract   A parcel of land; a piece of real estate.

Trade   1. Commerce.
2. A profession or business.

Trademark   A unique emblem that distinguishes the goods of a particular business; it is eligible for protection under federal law.

Transaction   The doing of some business; a dealing or the occurrence of some event between two parties.

Transcript   A copy; a complete record of a case taken from the court reporter's notes.

Transient   1. (adj) Temporary.
2. (n)   A person whose stay is temporary.

Treason   Attempting to overthrow the government or helping others to do so.

Treaty   A formal written agreement between nations.

Treble damages Triple damages; awarded in certain suits to discourage certain classes of wrongs.

Trespass A wrongful entry onto property; any wrongdoing. *See also* Criminal trespass.

Trespass on the case Common law action for injury resulting from anything but physical force, e.g., negligence, nonfeasance.

Trespass vi et armis *(Latin)* Literally, trespass with force and arms. A common law action for injury caused by direct force.

Trespasser A person who commits trespass.

Trial 1. A test.
2. A judicial proceeding.

Trial de novo *(Latin)* A new trial.

Tribunal A court.

Trover Common law action for recovering wrongfully taken or retained property.

True bill A grand jury indictment.

Trust A fiduciary relationship in which one party, the trustee, manages, holds, or controls some assets for the benefit of another, the beneficiary.

Trustee A person who holds property in trust for another.

Trustor A person who creates a trust; a settlor.

Turpitude Depravity; immorality.

U.C.C. *See* Uniform Commercial Code.

U.S.C. *See* United States Code.

U.S.C.A. United States Code Annotated.

Ultimatum A final offer.

Ultra *(Latin)* Beyond; in excess of.

Ultra vires *(Latin)* An act or contract that lies beyond the powers granted in the charter of a corporation.

Unconscionable Morally objectionable.

Unconscionable agreement or bargain An agreement or bargain made where one side has such a tremendous bargaining advantage and forces the other side to agree to such onerous term or terms that courts will not enforce the agreement or bargain.

Unconstitutional Contrary to the constitution.

Underwrite To insure.

Undue Unnecessary; inappropriate; more than needed.

Unequivocal Clear; certain.

Unfair labor practice An act by an employer which in any way coerces or intimidates employees who wish to organize for collective bargaining or in any other way violates a labor relations statute.

Uniform Commercial Code A comprehensive code regulating most aspects of commercial transactions. The U.C.C. has been adopted, at least partially, by almost every state.

Unilateral One-sided.

Union 1. A labor union; an association of workers for the purpose of collective bargaining.
2. Any merger or joining.

Union shop A place of employment where workers are required to become union members.

United States Code The codification of federal statutes.

Unjust Not rightful and proper.

Unjust enrichment Improper or unfair gain, the fruits of which are required to be returned to the rightful owner.

Unlawful Illegal; contrary to law.

Unlawful imprisonment The restraining of a person against his will.

Usage A usual course of conduct in a specific business.

Usurious Having to do with usury.

Usury The charging of illegally high interest rates on the loan of money.

V. versus.

Vacant Unoccupied.

Vacate 1. To set aside, annul.
2. To make vacant.

Vagrancy The state of being a vagrant.

Vagrant A person who moves about idly from place to place with no job or other source of income.

Vagueness Uncertainty; lack of precision.

Valid Legal; effective; operative.

Value Worth.

Variance 1. An exception from the effect of a zoning regulation.
2. A difference between the pleading in a case and the proof offered.

Vendee Buyer.

Vendor Seller.

Venire *(Latin)* The writ used to summon jurors.

Veniremen The panel of jurors.

Venue The locale where a case is to be tried. Where several courts may have jurisdiction, venue may be set at the most convenient for the parties. If venue is not properly set originally, it may be changed later.

Verdict The decision of a jury.

Verification A sworn statement that facts alleged in a document are true.

Verify To substantiate or conform; to make a verification.

Versus *(Latin)* Against.

Vest To take effect.

Vested In effect; no longer subject to conditions.

Violation A minor infraction, usually punishable only by a fine.

Vitiate To impair, weaken, or invalidate.

Viz. Contraction for videlicet *(Latin)*. That is to say; to wit.

Void Not valid; having no effect; null.

Voidable Capable of being voided or declared void.

Voir dire *(French)* Literally, to speak the truth. An examination of prospective jurors by the parties to see whether or not they are qualified.

Voluntary Of one's own free will.

Wages Salary, pay, or compensation for labor.

Waive To relinquish or disclaim.

Waiver The intentional relinquishment of a right or privilege.

Wanton Reckless; foolhardy.

Ward A person under care of an appointed guardian.

Warrant 1. (v) To promise.
2. (n) A form of process, e.g., arrest warrant. *See also* Search warrant.

Warrantor One who makes a warranty.

Warranty 1. A guarantee or promise that an allegation is true.
2. A promise by a vendor to indemnify against defects in what is being sold.

Waste Loss of assets through abuse of property by one who is lawfully in possession of it.

Wilful Voluntary; intentional; deliberate.

Will An instrument in which a person outlines the way in which his property is to be distributed after his death. It must be executed according to certain statutory formalities.

Witness 1. (v) To observe.
2. (n) A person who has observed a transaction; a person who testifies as to what he has observed.

Writ A process; an order of a judge either authorizing or requiring that something be done.

Wrong An infringement on a legal right.

Wrongful Unlawful; injurious; inequitable.

Zoning Division of a municipality into areas, or zones, with specific restrictions on the use of property within each zone. Serves to separate commercial property from residential.

Index

This index will enable you to locate all of the key words which appeared in italic type in the chapters. Simply look up the word that you wish to find and turn to the page number indicated.